AFTER THE LIGHT

What I Discovered on the Other Side
of Life That Can Change Your World

KIMBERLY CLARK SHARP

Authors Choice Press
New York Lincoln Shanghai

After the Light
What I Discovered on the Other Side of Life That Can Change
Your World

Authors Choice Press
an imprint of iUniverse, Inc.

For information address:
iUniverse
2021 Pine Lake Road, Suite 100
Lincoln, NE 68512
www.iuniverse.com

Originally published by William Morrow and Company, Inc.

ISBN: 0-595-28028-5

Printed in the United States of America

FOREWORD

▼

I THINK OF MYSELF as a sort of Everywoman, ordinary in just about every respect. You probably already know someone like me; that someone may even be you. Born in the heartland of America, reared in one of its comfortable, safe, postwar suburbs, I compiled a classic Baby Boomer vita—college educated, self-absorbed, and as middle class as they come. Though I had been planning and replanning my wedding since the age of eight, I put off marriage and children for a rewarding but exhausting career as a social worker at one of the busiest trauma hospitals on the West Coast. I became a bride and stepmother at thirty-eight, a mommy at forty, a cancer survivor at forty-two.

Like many of my generation, I've never been big on organized religion. I'm a lazy Lutheran. But I'm very spiritual. I believe with all my heart in Jesus, the Messiah, and the power of prayer. Angels, too. I know there is a higher being, wiser and better than we are, which will guide us if we let it. For lack of a better word, I call this force God; others may call it by other names: Yahweh, Allah, Buddha, or simply love. These differences don't matter to me. My truth doesn't have to be your truth. What is important, I think, is that we recognize the capacity for spiritual growth and awareness that exists in all of us, and that we learn to nurture it, for it in turn will nuture us. Soul food, so to speak.

How do I know this? The same way I know that these lives we live, with all their joy and sorrow, cares and tribulations, are flat and empty compared to "the other side"—beyond this earthly existence. It's hard to describe, since we have no words for the dimensions outside what we know as our "real life." Think of Charlie Brown and Snoopy in the comic strips. You can no more convey the experience of multiple dimensions—dimensions we have no name for—than you can tell a comic-strip character about the so-called real world. How could you possibly explain to Charlie Brown and his gang in comic-strip Flatland what it's like to be cold, be hungry, make love, bungee jump? By the same token, there's a gigantic difference between our own Flatland and life beyond. Everything there is clearer, fuller, more vital than the best day I've ever had on earth—and I've had some darn good days.

I didn't come by this knowledge in a book or at Sunday school. If I had, I wouldn't have believed it. Instead, I learned it the same way millions of people throughout history have, by coming so perilously close to dying that one visits the world beyond death. It happened to me on a spring day in 1970 when I collapsed outside an office in Shawnee Mission, Kansas. The electric impulse that regulates my heartbeat apparently misfired; I had no pulse and I wasn't breathing. My horrified father watched, helplessly, as strangers worked over my body and tried to revive me.

Though I was unconscious, I was completely aware of their efforts. In fact, I seemed to be aware of everything, from the sublime to the mundane. All of it flashed through my consciousness the way the landscape whizzes by when you're a kid in the backseat of a car. Here I was, an aimless twenty-two-year-old right out of college, being shown not only the meaning and purpose of life, but the entire range of emotions—anxiety, compassion, a little embarrassment—felt by the kind man whose mouth was pressed against mine as he gave me CPR on the pavement where I lay. But I wasn't there. I was on a journey, the most fantastic of my life.

In the days following my recovery, I didn't know what to think. There were no words in my vocabulary for what had happened to me, what I saw and felt on my strange journey to and from death. It didn't sound transcendent like I remembered—just crazy. If I tried to talk to my father about it, he became so emotional, it frightened me into silence. Something told me my friends wouldn't understand, either, so I didn't bring it up. In the file cabinet of my mind, the experience got shoved way, way to the back, hidden in a folder labeled WHEN I DIED.

Back in 1970, neither I nor anyone I knew had ever heard of a "near-death experience"—the term had not yet entered the popular lexicon. Dr. Elisabeth Kübler-Ross's new book, *On Death and Dying*, had barely begun to revolutionize our treatment of the terminally ill and challenge the scientific precept that consciousness ends with death. Others who later became pioneers in near-death research—among them, psychiatrist Raymond Moody and pediatrician Melvin Morse—were still students in medical school. It would be more than fifteen years before I became friends with a woman named Betty Eadie, whose book about her near-death experience sailed to the top of the best-seller lists. I was on my own, and I didn't have a clue.

What the conscious mind cannot grasp, the subconscious must muddle through. Outwardly, I was the same, but inside, a metamorphosis was taking place. Within weeks of my puzzling collapse, I made the boldest move of my (so far) predictable life: I packed up and headed west, leaving family, friends, and new fiancé behind in Kansas. After arriving in Seattle, I abandoned my career plans—I had studied to be a preschool teacher—and became a social worker instead. My workplace was Harborview Medical Center, one of the busiest trauma hospitals in the country, where I found myself face-to-face with death every day. All I knew was I needed to be there. P.M.H. Atwater, who has written extensively about the life-changing aspects of the near-death experience, estimates that it takes an average of seven years for the typical survivor "to even begin to integrate the experience within their lives." It was exactly seven years before I understood what had really drawn me to Harborview, and before I could share what had happened to me "when I died."

Now I realize that my NDE (near-death experience) had given me a mission, and that mission was to help others—the critically ill and their families, the bereaved, the fearful—deal with death. My work at Harborview and later as director of social work at Seattle's Fred Hutchinson Cancer Research Center coincided with a growing acceptance within the medical community of an uncharted gray area between clinically identifiable life and death.

This accepting attitude was by no means unanimous. A respected cardiologist once shouted at me that none of his patients had ever had an NDE. But from my bedside vantage point, the evidence was irrefutable. Eventually, I documented the cases of more than a thousand patients, including some of his, who lucidly described their near-death experiences. This research also confirmed that one need not come close to dying in order to experience elements of an NDE, such as out-of-body events, which some women report during normal childbirth.

After ten years as a clinical assistant professor on the faculty of the School of Social Work at the University of Washington, I still visit the classroom as a guest lecturer at the UW medical school and the department of psychology at Seattle University. Since 1981, I have traveled all over the country speaking to both medical professionals and lay persons on the subjects of sudden death, grieving, and the near-death experience. My work as co-founder and president of the Seattle International Association for Near-Death Studies (IANDS) has introduced me to Dr. Kenneth Ring, one of the foremost near-death researchers; Raymond Moody, Melvin Morse, Betty Eadie, and many others. I've also shared laughter, tears, hugs, and innumerable cookies with IANDS friends, whose support was essential to the writing of this book.

One of the aftereffects of visiting "the world beyond" is a heightened sensitivity to mystical, spiritual, even supernatural, occurrences. I've wrestled with a demon, conversed with ghosts, and been visited by angels. Sometimes I've seen the future before it happened. At Seattle IANDS we call such inexplicable phenomena "woo-woo" experiences—"woo-woo," we joke, is the sound the spiritual train makes right before it knocks us off the track. Strange stuff for a down-to-earth girl from Kansas, especially since the rest of my life is resolutely conventional. As I hurry off to work, drive in my car pools, schlepp the groceries, worry over children and bills, I sometimes recall these lines from an ancient poem by a Chinese Zen master:

> Before enlightenment, chop wood, carry water
> After enlightenment, chop wood, carry water

I've come to see our lives as a kind of school where we receive a series of lessons that prepare us for another, higher level of existence after this one ends. As Elisabeth Kübler-Ross has written:

> All the hardships that you face in life, all the trials and tribulations, all the nightmares and all the losses, most

people view as a curse, as a punishment by God, as something negative. If you would only realize that nothing that comes to you is negative. I mean nothing. All the trials and tribulations, the greatest losses, things that make you say, "If I had known about this I would never have been able to make it through," are gifts to you . . . an opportunity that you are given to grow.

We each grow and learn at our own pace, and some have harder lessons than others. They seem to be given extra work in grief, pain, loss, and suffering. I don't know why this is so, or why many of us tend to shirk our lessons and lose track of our assignments. But I believe a near-death experience is a wake-up call, affecting us like a *whump* on the back of the head from a big cosmic hand. "Pay attention!" the cosmic voice booms to the dazed student. And so we try.

Often, we still fail. But our capacity for learning, for awareness, is infinite. It does not end with death. Though our bodies will die, we—our essential selves—do not. We simply pass through another biological process, a shedding of tissue for which we have no further use. To truly understand that is to free ourselves from the shadow of death that darkens our earthly days. If we can overcome our fear of dying, we can get on with living. That's a lesson that should give us all hope, and strength.

ACKNOWLEDGMENTS

▼

A WALK-ON, in theatrical terms, is a member of the cast who usually has only a brief single appearance on stage. Yet when the actor "walks on" and delivers the lines, the whole play pivots and the plot takes a new, unexpected twist.

The walk-on for this act of my life was David Skinner. Working on a script treatment, he was stuck on how to present the nonfictional, central character's near-death experience. He looked up a friend he had not communicated with in many years. She was just the kind of extraspiritual person who might know about such things. She didn't, but she knew who did—former roomie and longtime playmate Kimberly Clark Sharp. Thank you, R. D., for giving David my name. And thank you, David Skinner, for recognizing the book I had within me and sending me off in the direction of others who would bring my story to publishing fruition. You are the book's godfather.

Thank you, Julie Blacklow, for playing an essential role in the earliest phase of this book's birthing. During the writing of the proposal, you got the words out of me and into your word processor. I also thank you for being such an effective taskmaster (although I'm still tender around the whiplash welts), for the sushi, and especially for bearing witness to the book's first appearance of invisible help.

It would add another hundred pages to the book if I listed all of the reasons for thanking my agents at Cine-lit Representation. In part, thank you for your unflagging support during the entirety of the process—accepting me as a client, framing and marketing the proposal, line editing the *thousand-page* first draft and most every draft thereafter, and digging me out the countless times I was buried in crises. Mary Alice Kier, the agent's agent, you are one of the precious few on earth capable of unconditional love. Thank you for always directing it my way. And thank you, Anna Cottle, for listening to me blather on in good times and bad. Your English accent makes the bitterest news seem like sweet wine.

Then there's the God squad. Gail Petitclerc laboriously transcribed and edited some thirty hours of dictation that was the template for the book. Then she spent every day for the rest of the year doing what I can't—getting my handwritten words onto the computer (yes, dear reader, I hand wrote this book because I'm computer illiterate). Thank you for your editing and clerical skills, your wise counsel, and for being my "gardening" angel.

Greg Wilson, the other God-squad member, is the hardest to thank because no helper was more devoted to the work. Greg, my right arm in Seattle IANDS, prayed aloud with me every day that the words would be God's words, the book, God's book. Thank you beyond measure for being my "able listener" during five months of dictation and my wordsmith during the several drafts that filled the remainder of that year. This book might be my story, but it belongs in almost equal share to you.

Then there's Brenda Bell. Like a literary Clint Eastwood, you rode into town, shot the fat off the book, stitched it back up tight as a girdle, then rode off without hardly saying a word. I've learned so much from you. Thanks, pardner.

Chris Fisher, thank you for your generosity in reading the first draft, listening to the dictated tapes, and drawing more insights out of me.

My editor and her assistant at William Morrow, Liza Dawson and Doris Cooper, probably look like unicorns by now for all the times they've banged their heads against walls when I wanted to add more content or said I was late. Liza, you get my special gratitude for always believing in the power of the book's message, coming up with the title, and using your considerable influence to get "The Swamp" published.

Those are the people whose fingerprints are on every page of the book, but there are many others whose special contributions made the writing possible. Thanks to the friends who provided childcare and car pools, especially Cathie Wong, Meredith Copeland, Lisa Gary, and Carolyn Robbins; and Staci Dao and Lynne Bradshaw for time spent on research.

My parents, David and Donnis Clark, spent many days relating the history of our family. Thank you for your truth, your boundless love, your prayers, and especially, thanks for having me. Thank you also to my brother, Paul Clark, and sister, Kristy Howell, and their families for prayers, emotional support, and jocularity. And thank you to my extended family, the Seattle International Association for Near Death Studies, for the monthly fix of highest positive energy, prayerful support, and hugs.

Last, I want to express my deepest gratitude to those closest to me: my stepkids, Andy and Jennifer, for your ongoing interest in the book even when you wanted to drop-kick me; to my beloved Rebecca for your patience and understanding at an age when you should have neither; to my life's partner, my sweet hubby and soul mate, Don, for the year of single parenting

while attending to a more-than-fulltime job, for the encouragement at my low ebbs and, more than anything, for loving me;
my "ghost writers," the unseen presences that surrounded me at
all times; and God, who made everything and everyone possible.

CHAPTER ONE

THE SHOE ON THE LEDGE

▼

B Y THE TIME I parked my green Volkswagen squareback in
the underground garage behind the hospital, the morning
sky was dark gray and it was raining horizontally. Winter
in Seattle is always wet, but usually, the precipitation falls in a
steady, soft drip that seasoned Seattleites such as myself—I'd been
living in the city for seven years—take pride in ignoring. Hori-
zontal rain, however, could not be ignored, and neither could its
effect on my Farrah Fawcett hairdo. I tried to plump some of the
wet mass back into shape. My shoulder-length mane, bleached
an amazing shade of white blond, was one of my vanities. It bil-
lowed in wavy curls that my patients called angel wings, because
from their bedridden perspective, the ceiling lights shining
through all that pale hair reminded them of a halo. Some of them
could have used a real angel, but I had to do.

Stepping out of the car in my inch-thick, rubber-soled Fa-
molare shoes and throwing my raincoat over my head, I braced
myself for The Gauntlet. That was my term for the route I had
to walk every day to get to work: a two-hundred-yard dash across
the ambulance parking lot, up the emergency driveway, through
the emergency room, and down the hall to my office on the first
floor of the hospital. It was always an interesting trip.

As I blindly splashed toward the hospital entrance, I heard the warning blast of an ambulance on its way out of the parking lot. I jumped out of the driver's path just in time to catch a waist-high shower of dirty water when the front tire hit a pothole. I broke into a run, ever mindful that I could become a hood ornament on the next ambulance to come barreling out of the dark rain. There was already a Medic One ambulance parked in front of the doors to the emergency room, where they were unloading an unconscious young man who was bleeding profusely.

"Anything for me?" I puffed, without breaking stride.

"Nah," said one of the medics. "He's going to surgery. Gunshot wound to the belly and head. Got a hole in his gut the size of Idaho. You comin' in?"

"After you," I said politely, slowing down and taking my raincoat off my head. As I started to follow the medics through the door, the belt buckle on my raincoat snagged on the back of the ambulance rig. It snapped me back like a fish on a line, landing me on my backside on the blood-splattered floor of the ambulance. With as much grace as I could muster, I lurched free and swept into the building, my hair a mess and a sopping, bloody raincoat flapping around my legs.

The usual cacophony of sounds greeted my entrance. The moans of people in pain mingled with the heaving groans of nausea. There was a chorus of drunken snores from "Gomers," Grand Old Men of the Emergency Room, lying in their gurneys, side by side. Occasional high notes—screams from the addicts and the mentally disturbed; cries of anguish from the bereaved—bounced off the institutional white walls. I hurried on.

Past the swinging doors of the ER, I entered the hall and was within sight of my office. I had made it through the rain and mud, blood and vomit. Then, only yards from the finish line, I watched a roving Gomer stagger up to the wall next to my door, take aim, and relieve himself upon it.

"Excuse me, sir, I'll just call someone about that," I murmured with a brisk nod toward the spreading puddle of urine composed, no doubt, of freshly recycled fortified wine. I ducked into my office, closed the door, and leaned heavily against it.

"Just another day in paradise," I announced to no one in particular, and threw back my head and laughed. "Geez, I love Harborview."

Like most of its patients, I arrived at the intensive care unit at Harborview Medical Center—Harborzoo, we called it, or simply The Zoo—by accident. As a graduate student in social work at the University of Washington, I'd written my thesis on child abuse and signed up for an internship with the young victims' section of the hospital's Sexual Assault Center. The internship fell through, and the consolation prize was a position with the intensive care units.

At first, I had protested the placement. My background was in early childhood education and child development. I knew nothing about medicine, nothing about the human body, nothing about illness and death. Heck, I hardly knew anything about grown-ups. But paid internships were hard to come by, so I took it anyway. It quickly became clear I had found my niche. I loved the crazy pace and high drama of life-and-death medical care. After hours, I took extra seminars in hospital social work, and boned up on the nomenclature of cardiology and respiratory disease so I could explain to patients what their doctors were talking about. My evaluations from my instructor, the nurses, and physicians were flawless. When the director of social work called me the Golden Girl of my group of interns, I couldn't have been prouder.

A teaching hospital for the University of Washington, Harborview's claim to fame was a trauma center serving a land mass one-fourth the size of the United States. The lights burned twenty-four hours a day in its high-energy emergency room, the regional critical care unit, and burn center. Critically ill and injured people were airlifted and brought in by ambulance from all over Washington, Idaho, Montana, and Alaska to this sprawling hospital atop "Pill Hill," on the steep rise east of downtown Seattle where most of the city's major medical facilities are located. With its busy heliport, constant ambulance traffic, and steady procession of troubled souls streaming in and out, you couldn't miss Harborview. Nor could you fail to notice that it also cared for the poorest, down-and-out sector of the city's population. Vagrants, drunks, runaways, prostitutes, the homeless, and mentally disturbed all found their way to Harborview, and often listed its address at 325 Ninth Avenue as their own when they applied for Medicaid.

The Zoo was truly paradise—for adrenaline junkies. The staff never walked when they could run. They didn't speak quietly, they shouted. The zaniness of the place and its characters made me feel like I had wandered onto the set for a hyped-up version of the television program M*A*S*H. Bank presidents and bums, diplomats and dumpster divers—everyone was thrown together and treated with the same degree of compassion and skill by professionals who didn't hesitate to bend rules to deliver the best medicine possible under the circumstances.

If you wanted to learn the ropes of social work, there was no better place than a big-city trauma hospital. I was taught by some of the best. Like Mary Bozarth—Miz Bozarth to you—the queen of 3-North, a floor primarily occupied by elderly or alcoholic (or both) patients. Mary was a big woman, with a manner so commanding that she could send a young pup of a medical intern scurrying out of his seat with a regal glance and the grave pronouncement, "Son, you're in my chair."

A tireless advocate for her patients, Mary knew how to cut through the bureaucratic red tape on their behalf. Many needed Medicare benefits or alcoholism treatment or nursing-home care, but were too out of it to sign the forms. They had no kinfolk or legal guardian to do it for them. So Mary would make a shaky X where the signature belonged, and sign her own name as witness to the mark. But when she really wanted action, she signed her notes on the patient's chart as simply "God." No one ever argued. When Mary finally retired, much to the dismay of the patients and staff who loved her, she was presented with two beautifully wrapped small packages. In each was an ink stamp. One was a shaky X. The other read GOD.

My own bailiwick on 2-North was the coronary care unit (CCU) and the medical intensive care unit (MICU). The first was for patients who had heart disease, heart attacks, and cardiac arrhythmias; the second housed patients with respiratory and renal failure, drug overdoses, and nonsurgical conditions that required ventilator assistance. Dr. Leonard Cobb was not only the heart and soul of CCU but also the creator of Seattle's nationally renowned emergency medical service, Medic One. His counterpart at MICU was Dr. Leonard Hudson, an expert on acute respiratory distress syndrome (ARDS), whose knowledge of respiratory function made him a virtuoso on the nose harp. My social work supervisor on these two high-intensity units was Jacqueline Durgin, a Hispanic woman who specialized in maintaining a calm demeanor in the face of chaos. Jacqueline lost her cool only once, to my knowledge, and that was the time she escorted a family to the morgue to view the body of a loved one. When she pulled out the drawer on which the corpse lay, it astonished everyone by sticking its head bolt upright—a rare quirk of rigor mortis brought on by a too tall man and a too short drawer. "My hair stood on end!" she told me. Considering that her black hair hung straight to her waist, that in itself would have been quite a sight.

It was invigorating to be associated with professionals of such high caliber, from the lowest, most inexperienced intern to the titans of medicine. Sure, there were plenty of wackos working at Harborview, but most of them were *dedicated* wackos, and their dedication was contagious. By the spring of 1977, I was helping teach a newly required course on terminal illness to second-year students at the School of Medicine, and had begun to seriously chart my course toward a faculty position at the School of Social Work. I loved teaching medical students, showing them how the little things made such a difference in patient care. For instance, it's an uncomfortable, vulnerable feeling to lie on a bed in a hospital gown while someone looms over you with a stethoscope and clipboard. Pull up a stool next to the bed, I urged the fledgling docs. Sit down and do your patients the courtesy of addressing them at *their* level.

From the perspective of The Zoo, my previous life in Kansas City seemed far, far away. I no longer felt like the same person who had left there in 1970, abandoning the predictable security of my upper-middle-class midwestern environment for the great unknown. I had a different home, a different career, different friends. I had even ditched my years of training in classical ballet and modern dance and joined a belly-dancing troupe! Most important, I related to people differently. At times, it seemed as if I were missing a layer of skin, a psychic barrier that both contains and separates us, and complicates our attempts to understand one another. To a degree I'd never believed possible, I could identify with people, including those I hardly knew, and intuit what they were thinking and feeling. Me, whose self-centeredness as a child, teenager, and young adult had known no bounds.

Empathy was invaluable in the work I had found after moving to Seattle: first as a housemother in a home for emotionally disturbed youth; then as a social worker specializing in abused children, and finally, in the Harborview job. It was at The Zoo, taking care of the unhealthiest patients, that I began to surprise myself. For some reason, I had a preternatural ability to calm ill or injured patients who were afraid of dying. I never examined my verbal—or perhaps it was nonverbal—communication style. Somehow, the right words just flew out of my mouth, allowing serenity and peace to envelop the final moments of my patients' lives.

There was no rational explanation for this gift. Everyone I had ever loved was still alive. Except for the episode I vaguely recalled as "when I died," death had not touched my personal life. If anyone had asked how I became so good at ministering to the needs of dying patients and their families, I would have been hard put to answer. On one level, I knew I had changed from the Kim Clark I used to be. On another, I had only a dim awareness of that change taking place. Perhaps I would have been able to do the mental archeology required to establish the event which signaled the beginning of my transformation. Maybe not.

At least, not until I met Maria.

Maria was a sinewy, middle-aged woman who had worked hard all her life, and now she was getting tired. A Hispanic migrant worker, she had been visiting friends in Seattle while her family continued to follow the crops in the Yakima Valley, two hundred miles to the east. Luckily for her, she had come in from the dusty fields to a city with excellent emergency medical care. Without warning, she suffered a massive heart attack and wound up in Harborview's CCU.

When I first met her, she looked sick, scared, and lost, hooked up to cardiac monitor wires from her chest to her calves, her long dark hair tangled on her pillow. I introduced myself and started in on the usual questions about family and finances. I tried to reassure her that we would find the money to help pay for her hospitalization; that we would find a way to contact her family; that she was in the best place she could possibly be, and that she was safe there. It wasn't clear how much she understood. But her English was better than my rusty high school Spanish, so we forged a kind of pidgin language that worked well enough. I told her she would get better, and she seemed to believe me.

Maria did get better. She pinked up as her circulation improved and her heart started to mend. We worked out the money issues and found her family. After three days in the coronary care unit, we were becoming friends. On the morning of the fourth day, I was having a cup of coffee and catching up on paperwork when a familiar, piercing alarm sounded, a signal that one of the patients was "flatlining"—in cardiac arrest. Through the window of the nurses' station, I could see the bank of glowing monitors which tracked the vital signs and cardiac activity of each patient. Inside, a nurse was calling a "code" on Maria.

Cardiac arrest codes were as common on 2-North as births in the maternity ward. Like the members of a practiced drill team, everyone knew where to go and what to do. I watched as a dozen different people—doctors, nurses, a respiratory therapist—took their places around Maria, who wasn't breathing. They thumped and massaged her chest with the palms of their hands, stuck tubes down her throat to bring air to her lungs, hooked her up to a portable electrocardiogram machine to measure her heart activity, and positioned the paddles to shock her heart into beating again.

I had seen plenty of resuscitations and knew this was an easy one. It took only a couple of shocks with the paddles to jump-start Maria's heart. She remained unconscious, but she was, in medical terms, in stable condition. I soon left on my rounds to see to my other patients. The next six hours proceeded routinely as I dealt with the usual assortment of family conferences and crisis interventions; searched for patients' next-of-kin; and arranged home health care for those who were leaving the hospital. Several hours after Maria's code, I was glad to hear she had regained consciousness and was breathing on her own.

But something was wrong. As I was getting ready to leave the hospital at about five o'clock, I got a call from the evening-shift nurse taking care of Maria. She said Maria was so agitated that she was afraid she would "flip back" into cardiac arrest. The nurse asked me to come see her immediately; Maria trusted me, and maybe I could calm her down.

When I got to the CCU, Maria was lying slightly elevated in bed, eyes wild, arms flailing and speaking Spanish excitedly. I had no idea what she was saying, but I went to her and grabbed her by the shoulders—in part to get her attention and calm her; in part to keep her in bed. She gulped air, panted, heaved her big bosom, and tried to collect herself. Our faces were inches apart, our eyes locked together, and I could see she had something important to tell me. But at that point, our pidgin language was not enough. Maria was struggling for words, for a language that didn't exist.

As she began to sob in frustration, I tried to bring her down with soft, quiet assurances. I told her I wouldn't leave her until I understood what it was she needed or was trying to tell me. "It's OK, it's OK," I said over and over as I gently stroked her arm.

"Take your time. Deep breath. Another deep breath. That's OK."
She slowly quieted down and began to talk, this time in words I
could understand.

Maria pointed to a corner of the ceiling and said she had
been up there watching people work over her body. She told me
precisely, and correctly, who had been in the room, where they
stood, what they did, and what they said. She described the placement of machinery and all the paper that had been kicked around
on the floor during the resuscitation, paper that the electrocardiogram machine had been continuously feeding out. Next, with
a snap of her fingers to show me how fast she had moved, Maria
told me she suddenly found herself outside the hospital room,
looking down at the emergency room entrance. She described
the curvature of the driveway, the vehicles all going in one direction and the doors opening automatically. Everything was absolutely accurate.

Then I did a curious thing. I refused to believe her. That is,
I knew the essential facts Maria was relating—the setting, the
sequence of events—were true. But my professional, rational
mind told me that Maria was "confabulating," that she was un-
consciously filling in the blanks of her memory with things she
made up because the human brain hates blank spots. That she
got the details right was due to information she had somehow
been privy to, and perhaps "forgotten." For instance, Maria's
room was located above the ER entrance. Somebody, probably
from housekeeping, must have pushed her bed next to the window in order to clean the room, and Maria saw the ambulance
traffic going by.

However, my theory ignored two obvious points. First,
never in my entire time on 2-North had I ever seen or heard
of anyone from housekeeping or any other department moving
a patient on life support in order to clean under a bed. Pa-

tients were literally plugged into wall and ceiling outlets, and were not easily rolled around just to mop the floor. Second, outside Maria's window was a huge, flat overhang that protected people from the omnipresent rain as they came in and out of the emergency entrance. The overhang blocked the view from Maria's room of all activity below.

Maria wasn't through yet. She said she had been distracted by something in a different part of the hospital, and she next remembered staring closely at an object on a window ledge about three stories above the ground. It was a man's dark blue tennis shoe, well-worn, scuffed on the left side where the little toe would go. The shoelace was caught under the heel. Maria was upset, she explained, because she desperately wanted someone to go get the shoe. Not to prove to herself that it was there; Maria knew she was an honest woman and she was telling the truth. No, she needed to prove it to others—that she really had been out of her body, floating free, outside the hospital walls. That she wasn't crazy.

She looked at me expectantly. It was clearly up to me to look for the shoe. Maybe she would feel better knowing that someone had believed her enough to make the attempt. Though I didn't really believe Maria, I did want to help her. As I left the hospital to begin this futile search, it dawned on me anew what a huge place Harborview was. Even if it *was* out there, how would I ever find a shoe on a ledge? I walked around the entire building and couldn't see a thing on any of the window ledges; from the ground, the tops of the ledges were largely blocked from view. OK, I'd tried. By now, it was way past quitting time, and I was ready to go home. But a small, clear voice inside me said to keep looking.

I decided to approach the problem systematically. I would have to go from room to room and inspect every window ledge;

it was the only way to satisfy my conscience and Maria, too. Back inside the building again, I started on the east side of the north wing on the third floor—Maria's wing. "Excuse me," I said with practiced officiousness to the occupants of each room as I made a beeline for the window. "I'm, uh, looking for something."

From the rooms on the east side, I saw nothing. On the north side—nothing. I was four rooms into the west side of the building when I pressed my face against a window pane, peered down on yet another ledge, and felt my heart go *thunk*. There it was.

Out on the narrow ledge below the window was a man's dark blue tennis shoe. It was well-worn, with the end of the lace tucked under the heel. I couldn't see if the little toe area was scuffed, because that side was facing away from the window. My gaze fell away from the tennis shoe, far away, toward the Olympic Mountains to the west and Elliott Bay spread out beneath them, forming a scenic backdrop for a lone high-rise building about a half-mile away. My mind raced through a dozen different explanations and settled on three possibilities.

According to the first scenario, Maria had earlier gained access to an upper floor of that high-rise building and with a telescope or binoculars had spotted the tennis shoe before she ever had her heart attack. The second explanation was that after coming to the hospital she had disconnected herself from life support, taken a tour of the third floor, slipped into a room and spied the shoe. The third was that Maria had taken a different sort of hike, at the very same time a dozen medical professionals had concurred that she was without cardiac or respiratory activity. While I had watched Maria's body being thumped and jolted, she—her sensory, aware self—was somewhere else.

I chose number three. That was Maria's amazing story. Equally astonishing, it was mine, too.

As I looked back at the shoe, my knees nearly gave out from under me. I leaned toward the window for support, my forehead still pressed against the pane. My breath fogged the glass as I slowly whispered, "This . . . happened . . . to . . . me."

It was as if a dark, empty spot in my memory had suddenly been exposed to the light. Images, clear images burst into my consciousness. I remembered voices, heard a woman cry out, "I'm not getting a pulse!" There was a strange fog, a condensation of light and dark particulate matter with the hazy quality of the Milky Way. After the haze there was light, a huge amount of light. Such light. I wanted to stay there forever. But I was told I had to leave. "Go back. Go back." Then there was my body. My God! *I had watched my body!*

The light, the presence spoke to me again. Not really in a voice—more like a message, a message I understood without actually hearing it. The words of the message were: "You will forget everything except as it will be manifest." *Forget everything.* I had forgotten, in a way. Now I remembered, in a flood, a rush of feelings that overwhelmed me.

Carefully, I opened the window and reached out for the shoe. I wondered if it would dissolve, fade out as in a dream. It didn't seem real. But now the shoe was in my hand. It had weight and substance, and truth. It validated Maria and it validated me. And it might validate others who had died and remembered it. There were at least two of us, and I knew there had to be more. I also knew I worked in the perfect place to find them.

The world came back into focus, clearer than I had ever perceived it. A decision was taking shape in my mind. This was a new direction and I had to be willing to follow it wherever it led me. I would search for and talk with people who had had this experience, whatever it was called. I wanted them to know that they weren't alone, and that what they had experienced was real—as real as this shoe on a ledge of a hospital in the middle of a city in the shadow of the mountains.

Turning the shoe slowly in my hands, I noticed one more thing. On the side where the little toe would fit, it was very scuffed.

Now it was my turn to be agitated. Holding the shoe and trying to get a grip on my unruly emotions, I made my way back to 2-North and Maria.

When I walked into Maria's room, I hid the tennis shoe behind my back. Not to tease her, but to stall for time to ask one more question. Did she remember what the inside of the shoe looked like? "No," Maria replied. She explained she had not been quite high enough to see inside the shoe from above, but was at eye level with the side of the shoe facing away from the building. It was a perspective, I realized, that would only be possible from midair, three stories above the ground.

"¿Por qué?" Maria asked. Why did I want to know?

"Because," I answered, "I couldn't see the shoe at all from the ground, and when I looked down on it from inside, all I could see was the top and inside." Triumphantly, I whipped out the shoe from behind my back.

"Oh, my God! ¡Diós mío!" Maria cried, beside herself with bilingual joy. "The shoe! ¡Lo encontraste! You found it! ¡El zapato! ¡Gracias, gracias! Oh, thank you!"

A nurse scurried in to find out why Maria's heart rate was popping like a Mexican jumping bean on the cardiac monitor. Excitedly, we pointed to the shoe and told her everything from beginning to end—how Maria had been in cardiac arrest and saw the shoe and how I had found it later. Well, almost everything.

I didn't bring up the flashback to my own, similar experience. The time wasn't right, and I just wasn't ready yet for the inevitable questions.

By the next morning, every nurse in the CCU knew Maria's story, and by afternoon, a parade of doctors and nurses and other staff members had dropped in to pay their respects to the humble shoe. Maria displayed the shoe on a side table in her room, and received her many visitors with gracious hospitality. They saw, they touched, they left. No one, at least in the company of Maria or me or members of her resuscitation team, disputed a word of her account. Too many knew the seriousness of Maria's condition, and realized how impossible it would have been for her to have had detailed foreknowledge of the shoe.

On the day she was to be discharged from the hospital, I dropped by. I was relieved to find Maria alone for once. Ever since the incident with the shoe, I had wanted to tell her about the time "when I died" seven years earlier. I wanted her to know that I understood, truly understood what she had felt. It was now or never.

Dressed in her going-home outfit, with her hair freshly brushed and her lipstick on, Maria looked younger than when we had first met only two weeks ago. She sat on the edge of the bed as I talked to her, and her eyes grew wider and wider. She couldn't believe that we shared this—this *what*? Maria didn't know what to call this experience, and neither did I. All she knew was that she had come very close to dying, and in that process, journeyed to another dimension which was neither life as she knew it nor death as she had been taught it would be. When I finished talking, Maria reached for the blue shoe, the souvenir of that journey. She handed it to me.

"Here," she said quietly. "You keep it."

And I did, for a long time. Had I known that Maria's story

would eventually become the best-known among contemporary accounts of out-of-body experiences, I would have kept better tabs on the shoe—and Maria, too, for that matter. After she relocated in Seattle to be near its medical services, we kept in touch for a few years, then she dropped out of sight. As for the shoe, it slipped away during one of my moves from one house or another, and it never turned up again, either.

Maria's most important gift to me wasn't the shoe, anyway. It was the validation of the reality of my own experience "when I died"—an experience I either couldn't or wouldn't come to terms with when it happened. That confirmation in turn led to an awakening and expansion of spiritual faculties I already had, but wasn't sure what to do with. Oh, sure, I had a knack for saying the right words and doing the right things for my patients. But in a spiritual sense, I was also like a kid with a great jump shot who barely knew how to play basketball. Not yet thirty years old, I still had a lot to learn.

According to countless adults who've been there, a near-death encounter not only triggers a sweeping review of one's life, but of one's past failures and mistakes. The universal response is an exercise in wishful thinking. We wish we had said or not said this; we wish we had done or not done that; we wish we had been truer to ourselves. At the same time, we realize that we are not being reprimanded or condemned for our shortcomings. We are simply learning.

CHAPTER TWO

MAY DAY MAYDAY: MY NEAR-DEATH EXPERIENCE

▼

FOR THE FIRST twenty-two years of my life, spirituality was the last thing on my mind. My family comes from a long line of strivers—practical Scottish and German agrarians with their feet firmly planted on the midwestern earth. The land was their salvation. Poverty drove my father's grandparents from Scotland, and famine squelched their future in Ireland. Like millions of Europeans during the nineteenth century, they came to America with empty pockets, a few battered belongings, and dreams of prosperity. Their hopes were realized in the rich, loamy soil of central Iowa, which was productive beyond belief. Their youngest son, my grandfather, married a local girl, also from immigrant stock, and together they raised corn and kids. When my grandfather was fifty-three and my grandmother was forty-three, they received a midlife surprise: their seventh and last child, whom they named David. He was my dad.

During the Depression, the Clark family temporarily lost the farm and their newfound prosperity, and became tenant farmers on their own land. My father's wardrobe consisted of hand-me-downs from his six siblings, and he never got over the embarrassment of going to school wearing his sister's old shoes. That was what motivated him the rest of his life: his fear of losing the farm, losing it all. No kid of mine, he vowed, would ever have to wear his sister's *or* brother's shoes to school.

Compared to plowing Iowa dirt, fighting in World War II looked like a better deal to David Clark. He joined the marines and spent three years in the Pacific theater. On Okinawa, he caught a Japanese bullet in his left thigh, followed by shrapnel from an exploding mortar which ripped open his side and belly. Placed in the field hospital tent reserved for those whose wounds were likely fatal, he made another vow: to live, to walk, to "make it."

He met my mother, Donnis Lueking, through her letters. She had been writing to her cousin in the marines, who showed her letters to my dad. On a lark, he wrote her back. They had been corresponding for a year when my father was evacuated to a navy hospital in San Francisco. On his first medical liberty, he flew to Kansas City to meet the girl whose face he had seen only in a photograph. Three days later, she accepted his proposal of marriage.

Donnis Lueking was itching for some adventure of her own. Willful and free-spirited, she chafed under the religious and academic strictures of her reorganized Latter Day Saint mother and the iron hand of her German Lutheran father, another farmer's son. Unfortunately, marriage and motherhood didn't turn out to be quite the liberation she had sought. The year I was born, 1948, was the year my father plunged into his law studies at Stanford University. Soon after he graduated, my mother had two more babies and a clearer view of what her future held. By then, our family had reestablished itself in Kansas City, where my father's dogged aspirations and my mother's thwarted expectations formed the leitmotiv of our good life in the suburbs.

My brother and sister and I grew up in Leawood, one of the most affluent suburbs in America, in a household whose members were kind but largely oblivious to one another. As a workaholic partner in a major Kansas City law firm, my father was seldom home. My artistically inclined mother was often absent, too, socializing with a crowd of interior designers and their friends, whose conversation was infinitely more interesting than the cocktail-party chitchat at my father's country club. What we may have lacked in parental attention, we children received in other things: clothes, dance lessons, horseback riding at a nearby stable, and all the play pretties money could buy. Instead of being involved with my younger siblings, I was distant and selfish, with no responsibility for their care and little interest in what they were doing. None of us even noticed that my little brother, a musical genius who had his own rock-and-roll band in junior high, was zonked on drugs throughout his adolescence. Like residents of a very nice hotel, we nodded to each other at the front desk and went our separate ways.

The only breaks in my self-centered routine were when my maternal grandmother, Tyra Lueking, dragged my sister and me into Kansas City on her regular charity rounds. Tyra was an amazing woman. Though almost completely deaf, she marched right into urine-soaked nursing homes, unkempt shelters for the handicapped, and dismal slums, where she generously dispensed food and affection. Though we sometimes didn't know what to make of these people and their shabby surroundings, we thoroughly enjoyed these excursions because we loved being with my grandma.

By the time I graduated in 1970 from Kansas State University, shortly after my twenty-second birthday, the future looked like smooth sailing—in a very sheltered harbor. At KSU, the rules included curfews, dorms segregated by gender, and a dress code for women that prohibited the wearing of pants unless the temperature dipped below freezing. The larger political issues of the day—Vietnam, Cambodia, racial conflict, women's liberation—caused tidal waves in places like Berkeley and Madison, but barely ruffled the surface of our placid college campus in Manhattan, Kansas. We had more important concerns, like marriage.

My major was in family and child development, with a minor in special education—a classic girl's degree. Though I had no idea what to do with my education, it didn't matter; the assumption was that my husband would take care of me, just as my father had done. Most of my friends were either married, getting ready to be married, or worried about not being married. I had that covered, too. I was planning to marry Bob Clark, a boy I'd known since junior high school. It pleased me that I wouldn't even have to change my name when I became his wife. I hated change of any sort.

But change was exactly what was in store for me that morning in May as my father and I drove to the nearby town of Shawnee Mission in eastern Kansas. It was the kind of balmy spring day that does the Midwest proud—a perfect blend of warm sun, cool breeze, and brilliant blue sky. Our destination was the Department of Motor Vehicles office, where we would register and pay the license fee for my first car. As a graduation and birthday present, my parents had given me the down payment for the vehicle of my choice—a green squareback Volkswagen. More accurately, it was Bob Clark's choice because it was a practical car and got good gas mileage. Deferential to a fault, I let him pick it out. If I had any other preference myself, I do not remember it.

There wasn't a long line inside the DMV office, but for some reason, I felt impatient. It seemed awfully stuffy in the large room. I began to feel dizzy, and quickly became so light-headed that I turned to my father and told him I wanted to sit down. He looked around, saw that all the seating was occupied, and said, "Gee, Chick, there aren't any chairs."

Certain scenes from our lives are indelibly fixed in our memory, and this is one of mine. I remember smiling through my wooziness at my dad's affectionate childhood nickname for me. I remember how the bright sunlight from the windows and fluorescent light from the ceiling fixtures cast odd shadows around the room with its institutional furnishings. I remember a few casually dressed people standing around looking bored as they, like us, waited for their number to be called. After that, the scene blurs.

My father recalls, because I do not, what happened next.

In probably ten to fifteen minutes, our number was called and we moved forward to the designated window. Kim was still complaining about not feeling good, but I persuaded her that we should soon be finished . . . I was under the impression Kim was doing all right because she appropriately signed the various documents and took the receipts.

Just before we reached the door to the exit, Kim said she couldn't catch her breath. It was then, for the first time, that I became cognizant of her facial coloring, almost white on white. As we stepped outside, she collapsed. I was holding her by the left arm so she did not fall hard. But her weight was dead weight and I was unable to keep her from going down. She fell into and through my arms.

There was a confusion of people because Kim had fallen in front of the adjacent entrance door, blocking both doors with her body. I didn't know what to do and was so relieved when a young woman in a white nurse's uniform knelt beside Kim. My relief changed to panic when she said she could not find Kim's pulse and told someone to call the fire department. It seemed two volunteer firemen arrived almost instantly. One was carrying a portable ventilator machine and one of them commented that it was the first time they'd used it since its recent purchase.

Kim wasn't breathing. The woman in the white uniform moved away. Time stood still. Kim was totally out. I saw my daughter lying there as helpless as I felt. I watched the firefighters hook Kim up to the machine and then argue about which end to apply to her mouth and nose. How long this argument continued, I do not know. It seemed like forever when another man suddenly burst onto the scene. I think he was also a fireman and he swore like a muleskinner. He literally threw the two men on the sidewalk and yelled, "You've even got the pressure going the wrong way! She'll never breathe!"

He put his ear to her heart and then started pounding Kim's chest and giving her what I now know, but did not then, as CPR. Again, I don't know how long that went on. I was in a fog and some people helped me sit down. I couldn't see her anymore—my only recollection is of hoses and men's legs. Occasionally, a voice would say, "I can't get a pulse," and another voice would say, "I can." Suddenly, there was a yell, then more yells, and people were clapping.

At some point during the resuscitation—I don't know when—an ambulance arrived. One of the ambulance personnel assured me that Kim had been revived, that she would probably be all right, but they would nevertheless have to take her to a hospital for observation. I asked if I could go with them. At no time during the ride did Kim appear to be conscious, but her chest was rising up and down. I asked the attendant if she was breathing on her own. He said yes. They were still applying oxygen, but her pulse was almost normal.

At the hospital, Kim was taken by gurney from the ambulance to the emergency room. I was asked about her medical history, especially of unconsciousness or fainting, and whether or not she had experimented with drugs, to all of which I replied in the negative. After examination, she was placed in one of the curtained areas in the emergency room. It was then that I first looked at my watch and realized more than one and a half hours had passed.

I sat beside Kim for a while, and she appeared to sleep. I'd call her name from time to time but got no response. I actually was afraid to touch her. After a while, two doctors came in and were able to rouse Kim. She opened her eyes, which they examined with small flashlights. The doctors told me that they thought Kim would be all right, but they wanted to keep her in the emergency room a couple of more hours. For the first time, Kim looked at me and asked, "Dad, are you OK?" All of us laughed at that.

Afterwards, over the next few years, three or four times, Kim would ask me to relate what happened. I told her bits and pieces but tried to get off the subject as quickly as possible, as each time it revived in me the guilty feeling of helplessness. It was not until several years later that Kim first told me of her near-death experience.

This recollection is my father's memory, my father's reality, my father's pain and grief—my father's experience. It's not mine, because I wasn't there. I was somewhere else.

The first thing I remember after hearing there were no chairs where I could sit was the urgent sound of a woman's voice. "I'm not getting a pulse!" she said. "I'm not getting a pulse." Though I don't remember actually seeing her, I turned in her direction and said, with some irritation, "Of course you're getting a pulse or I wouldn't be speaking!" But she ignored me and continued to talk about my pulse. This made no sense. Again, speaking very slowly for emphasis, I corrected her. "You *must* be getting a pulse or I wouldn't be *speaking.*"

In fact, I said, I felt fine. Really good. Come to think of it, I'd never felt better, or more alive. I was healthy and whole, calm and together for the very first time in my life. Though I still couldn't see, I could hear everything—mostly the scramble of many voices talking all at once—but especially the tone of worry in the woman's voice. It didn't bother me. Nor was I offended by everyone's refusal to listen to me or notice that I was OK. I let it go. I let everything go.

It was easy to give up and be quiet, easy to surrender. I just slipped away, as if I was falling asleep without being drowsy first. I had no fear, no sense of alarm or panic. It was like being carried someplace that was inviting, comfortable, and safe—like my warmest childhood memories of being carried to bed by one of my parents. There was that same sense of security, of being taken to a place where I could rest, and be cared for. Where I would be loved.

My next awareness was of an entirely new environment. I knew I was not alone, but I still couldn't see clearly, because I was enveloped in a dense, dark gray fog—not a cold fog but a warm one. I was grateful for that; despite my years in Kansas, or perhaps because of them, I despise the cold. I felt a sense of expectancy, the same anticipation one feels waiting for a plane to take off or arrive. It seemed natural and right to be here, and for

AFTER THE LIGHT

me to wait as long as it took. Earthly time had no meaning for
me anymore. There was no concept of "before" or "after." Everything—past, present, future—existed simultaneously.

I realized that I could discern the particles that made up the
fog. I could perceive individual glints of penetrating light and
droplets of unfathomable darkness. It wasn't black and white
makes gray—it was just light and dark, without color. I could
focus on one, then the other, and perceive different patterns, like
a 3-D painting.

Suddenly, an enormous explosion erupted beneath me, an
explosion of light rolling out to the farthest limits of my vision.
I was in the center of the Light. It blew away everything, including the fog. It reached the ends of the universe, which I could
see, and doubled back on itself in endless layers. I was watching
eternity unfold.

The Light was brighter than hundreds of suns, but it did not
hurt my eyes. I had never seen anything as luminous or as golden
as this Light, and I immediately understood it was entirely composed of love, all directed at me. This wonderful, vibrant love
was very personal, as you might describe secular love, but also
sacred. The only words I could formulate in the midst of this
incredible Light were from my childhood: "Homey home." It was
something I used to say when we had been on an outing and I
began to spot the familiar landmarks of our neighborhood.

Though I had never seen God, I recognized this light as the
Light of God. But even the word God seemed too small to describe the magnificence of that presence. I was with my Creator,
in holy communication with that presence. The Light was directed at me and through me; it surrounded me and pierced me.
It existed just for me.

The Light gave me knowledge, though I heard no words. We
did not communicate in English or in any other language. This

was discourse clearer and easier than the clumsy medium of language. It was something like understanding math or music—nonverbal knowledge, but knowledge no less profound. I was learning the answers to the eternal questions of life—questions so old we laugh them off as clichés. "Why are we here?" To learn. "What's the purpose of our life?" To love. I felt as if I was rerembering things I had once known but somehow forgotten, and it seemed incredible that I had not figured out these things before now.

Then this ecstasy of knowledge and awareness was interrupted. Again, without words, I learned that I had to return to my life on earth. I was appalled. Leave all this, leave God, go back to that old, oblivious existence? No way. The girl who always did as she was told dug in her heels. But to no avail. I was going back. I knew it. I was already on the way. I was on a trajectory headed straight for my body, that lifeless lump on the sidewalk in front of the Department of Motor Vehicles.

I didn't quite make it. Maybe it was my resistance to going back, maybe it was just that I've never been good with spatial orientation. I'm so inept at parallel parking that if I can get the car within four feet of the curb, I consider it a victory. It was the same for parking my soul back into my body. I missed by a good four feet.

That's when I saw my body for the first time, and when I realized I was no longer a part of it. Until this moment, I'd only seen myself straight on, as we usually do, in mirrors and photographs. Now I was jolted by the strange sight of me in profile from four feet away. I looked at my body, the body I knew so well, and was surprised by my detachment. I felt the same sort of gratitude toward my body that I had for my old winter coat when I put it away in the spring. It had served me well, but I no longer needed it. I had absolutely no attachment to it. Whatever constituted the self I knew as me was no longer there. My essence, my consciousness, my memories, my personality were outside, not in, that prison of flesh.

Then I watched a man lean over that body and put his mouth to mine. That instant of physical contact was all I needed. This man became the conduit that I passed through on the way to my own body, and for a brief moment, I was observing as well as experiencing what was happening to us both. I realized I knew everything about him emotionally. I could feel his nervousness and even his discomfort about performing this intimate, humane service in front of a gawking crowd. But it was his compassion, his love for me, a total stranger, that guided me—unerringly this time—back into my body.

(Fade to black. Fade to blacker.)

I heard a woman calling my name, and though I wanted to respond, I could not answer her. I wanted to go toward her voice, but it took too much effort. I was cold now, cold from the inside out, like a corpse. I felt as if I were moving through a dank, dark hallway blocked by heavy tapestries that I desperately tried to push aside, to get to that voice. But I was getting nowhere.

A window opened up on my right and fresh air blew into this horrid place. Through the window, I saw a beautiful pastoral scene, like a calendar photograph of a Kentucky meadow: emerald grass and brilliant white fences under intensely saturated blue skies. Somehow, I knew that all I had to do, if I wanted to die, was slip through the window into that bucolic beauty. If I went, I would not come back this time. I decided to go through the window.

But at this very moment, I was made aware of the potential

KIMBERLY CLARK SHARP

my life would have if I chose to continue it. I saw that there could be a larger purpose for my life—that I could accomplish considerable good and be of service to many people. It was an offer I could not resist.

I chose life.

As I began to regain consciousness, I received one last message. A male voice spoke a single sentence—the only clear words, besides "Homey home," that I could initially retrieve from my memory of this incredible journey. The voice said I would forget everything "except as it will be manifest."

The message threw me. If I could have, I would have reached out, grabbed my messenger by the shoulder, and spun him around. "What are you talking about?" I would have asked. "What does manifest mean? And why do I have to forget? *What* am I supposed to forget?"

The ambulance ride was uneventful, according to my father. I wouldn't know. It's as if a giant eraser wiped away my memory of the rest of the day. After having been infused with cosmic knowledge and universal understanding, having felt the presence of God and experienced unconditional love, I recall nothing else. If I contemplated my transcendent experience, or made mental notes on the wisdom I had gained, I don't remember it. Physically and psychically drained, I slipped into unconsciousness. Wisdom would have to wait.

CHAPTER THREE

WE'RE NOT IN KANSAS ANYMORE, TOTO

▼

A FTER A THOROUGH EXAMINATION and several hours of observation in the emergency room of St. Luke's Hospital in Kansas City, I was sent home with a pat on the shoulder but no clear explanation for my collapse. The doctors said I might have suffered a once-in-a-lifetime bout of cardiac arrhythmia—a wild fluctuation in heartbeat. Or maybe I had simply fainted and experienced a severe drop in blood pressure. Either diagnosis was complicated by the length of time I had gone without oxygen during the snafu with the portable ventilator. Fortunately, the doctors assured me, there seemed to be no lasting effects. It turned out they were wrong, but I didn't know that at the time.

My family didn't make a fuss about my brush with death. Only my dad knew the whole story, and he wasn't talking much. When I tried to approach him to discuss "when I died," he got choked up and changed the subject. Anyway, I had reasons of my own for letting this particular sleeping dog lie. My secret fear was that something awful had happened to me following my collapse— something neither my dad nor I could do anything about. I was afraid I had gone crazy.

Not lunatic crazy. Just a little "off." The first thing I noticed after the incident was that I immediately felt different. It was a subtle but distinct change—as if I had stepped out of the house to run a quick errand, and someone had rearranged the furniture ever so slightly in my absence. Nobody seemed to notice except me. This feeling of things being amiss was exacerbated by the fact that I had undergone an experience for which I had no words. My recollections were muddled, consisting of images and emotions that made no literal sense, but seemed loaded with meaning and power. Yet I could not describe them.

Later, I learned that this inability to translate these images into words is characteristic of the near-death experience. It's called ineffability. It means, simply, that which cannot be spoken, which language cannot describe. I discovered this when I tried to tell my grandfather, Fred Lueking, about what had happened to me, and burst into great racking sobs instead. He pulled me into his lap and patted me with his huge soft hands, trying to comfort me as if I were a child again. But comfort was hard to come by. Overwhelmed and confused by the haunting memory of something I could not quite grasp and changes I could not explain, I took to staring at myself in the mirror, slowly turning my head first this way, then that, until I was almost in profile. My eyes followed my reflection in the glass, as if I could find the clues to the mystery there.

Remember, this was Leawood, Kansas, in 1970. No one knew what a near-death experience was, or even what to call it. There were no books, television programs, movies, or lectures on the subject. There was no road map, no frame of reference, no guide of any sort. My head echoed with the cryptic message that I would forget everything "except as it will be manifest." I looked up "manifest" in the dictionary and read this definition: "evident, obvious, apparent." Great. The only thing obvious to me was that I was in pain. Edgy and restless, I began to examine the predictable pattern of my life the same way I studied my face in the mirror. I wanted out.

Relationships that had previously felt secure now felt confining. I perceived my relationship with my fiancé, Bob Clark, as smothering. I perceived my relationship with my family and friends as smothering. I perceived my relationship with the state of Kansas as smothering. This didn't feel like a delayed adolescent rebellion, or a loss of love for the people and places I had cared for. It was as if I were expanding so rapidly that I was literally bursting through the shell of my previous existence, and I was simultaneously being pulled away by a force that was greater than my love for family, friends, Kansas, or Bob. Although I didn't specifically identify the force as God, it had a quality that I now recognize as spiritual. Underneath the feeling of being stifled was the sense that I was being called. To what, I didn't know. But I had an idea about where.

During spring break of my senior year in college, I had flown out to Seattle to visit a friend. This was wildly exciting for me, since I'd never traveled anywhere by myself. As the plane descended and broke through the cloud cover, I could see snow-capped mountains and water from both sides of the aircraft, and more towering green trees than existed in all of Kansas. The landscape was no less exotic to me than Bombay or Bali, and suggested equally mysterious possibilities. Was Seattle really only two thousand miles from home? It felt like two million. Now I was increasingly eager to put that distance between me and Leawood again.

Click, click, click; everything fell into place as if I had been planning for months to move away. My college friend Mary Sue Bollig also wanted to leave her hometown of Hays, Kansas. Under the guise of a temporary sojourn, not a permanent relocation, we planned to pack up and drive west together in my new Volkswagen, which I dubbed the Green Weenie. My mother thought I was running away from home for a while and would soon be back. But I knew I was running *to* something, not away. And I certainly didn't feel I had chosen the easy path. Easy would have been marrying Bob and becoming Mrs. Kim Clark. Hard was watching Bob, my family, and the dog sadly waving good-bye from the front yard.

That's why I had a lump in my throat as I backed the Green Weenie out of the driveway on the day of departure, only two weeks after my collapse at Shawnee Mission. Clumsily shifting gears—I still didn't know how to drive a stick shift properly—I waved my own sad good-byes as the Green Weenie lurched down the street. Next to me on the passenger seat with a seat belt strapped snugly around his cage was my hamster, Toto. My seat belt was fastened, too. We were ready for the tornado, Oz, the whole shebang.

Interstate-70 West, the road I took to pick up Mary Sue in Hays, a toll road. As I pulled up to the toll booth, a sign advised motorists that change was needed. *Change?* I despised change and now it had commandeered my life. How did this happen? Driving through Topeka and Manhattan, where I'd gone to college, I ticked off the familiar landmarks one by one. But once past the last exit to campus, I was in unfamiliar territory and the full weight of my decision to leave home lay heavily on my heart. Before I knew it, I was crying. What was I doing out here in the middle of nowhere, putting seventy miles per hour between me and everything I'd ever known? Was I nuts? And where was my Kleenex? My emotional crisis had led to the inevitable need for tissues.

Frantically, I pawed through my purse and around the front

seats with one hand but couldn't find a thing to blow my nose with, which made me blubber even more. The highway blurred through my tears. I let out a loud, long wail and rested my forehead on my forearms across the top of the steering wheel. The same way you might lay your weary head down on a desk, but not—if you had any sense—the steering wheel of a moving car. I didn't care. I squeezed my eyes shut and wailed, "Please, God. Help me. Please help me. I don't know what I'm doing." This would have been painfully obvious to anyone, much less God. What confidence I had in this bold endeavor of mine had rapidly dissipated. Fearful of the unknown, of *really* being on my own, I cried and cried.

But soon a sense of calm came over me. I realized that even though I wasn't steering or keeping my foot steady on the accelerator, the car maintained a constant highway speed and stayed in the same lane. It was as if a separate entity was in control, as if Toto and I were being chauffeured by an invisible, comforting presence. I leaned full back into the seat, taking staccato gasps of breath as my sobs subsided, and let the calmness wash over me. I wiped away my tears with the backs of both hands confident that the car would continue safely forward without my full attention. Then I looked down between the front seats. On the floor next to my purse sat a full box of tissues, the first white tissue already pulled out of the slot. Beneath the brand name, in a print style so large that it dominated the package was the name of the manufacturer, which happened to be the same as my own: Kimberly Clark.

There was still another sign to come. It began to take shape later in the afternoon, as the clouds piling up in the sky took on an ominous pale green hue. In Kansas, in June, this was a portent of hail or a tornado or both. Growing up in Tornado Alley, you learn to read this sort of weather the same way that I imagine an

KIMBERLY CLARK SHARP

Eskimo discerns the color and texture of various kinds of snow. You can judge the likelihood of a twister by the darkness, shape, and movement of the clouds, the direction of the wind, the proximity of the thunder and lightning, the feel of the air—you can tell when the barometric pressure is dropping too fast. I sniffed the air and checked the clouds, and determined that what we had here was a good old thunderstorm in the making. There would be no tornado.

Imagine my surprise when a funnel suddenly dipped down from a mogul-shaped cloud to the south of eastbound I-70. I thought my heart would jump right out of my chest and crawl into the cage with Toto. I had seen very few twisters in my life, because we always took shelter below ground when the air-raid sirens blasted a tornado warning. "Duck and cover" had no nuclear connotations in the Midwest; we hid not from the flash, but from the wind.

But after giving this particular funnel cloud a closer look, I relaxed. Instead of a mean, snarling mass of destruction, this was a rather dainty thing as tornadoes go—tall, thin, elegant. We called such cyclones *dust devils*. They were more likely to tear the laundry off the line than the roof off the house. Once I realized this twister was not going to suck me out of the car and deposit me somewhere in Nebraska, I began to admire its form. It looked like a thin swirl of silver cotton candy spun out from verdigris clouds, narrowing down to a snakelike tail that whipped across the landscape, churning great billows of dust from fallow fields.

I was in awe of its beauty, its grace. With a sense of heightened awareness that was new to me, I realized that this tornado and I had much in common. We were both westbound, traveling side by side at a high rate of speed and in a state of controlled chaos, guided by an invisible force. As it cleared a path along the ground, kicking up dirt like chalk dust from an eraser, so was I

34

sweeping away the plans I had once made for my life. I felt a deep understanding and respect for this whirling dervish of energy, which also had a life of its own. Simultaneously, I realized that the twister's appearance at this time and place was no accident; that there are no accidents in life; that everything, no matter how random or serendipitous, is in fact interconnected and purposeful. Later, I would come to recognize this feeling, which I have since experienced hundreds of times, as a reminder of the awakening that marked "the time I died." Reactions of near-death experiencers vary from individual to individual, but one of the most common aftereffects is the strong belief that life has meaning, that there is a plan for us. This was the first of many, many occasions when the realization of this connectness would comfort and sustain me.

For now, it was enough to know that Toto and I had made it safely through another crisis. Let's see—we were only a few hours out of Kansas City. How many more potential calamities would there be? Funny, the prospect didn't alarm me anymore. It invigorated me instead. When you thought about it, I was one lucky gal—alive, healthy, and on the road in my own car, taking my own risks, learning my own lessons. All I needed was a pal to share this adventure with, and to find the Kleenex when I needed it. So I was thrilled to see the highway signs that announced the city limits of Hays, a prairie oasis of green trees and silos. Veering off at the next exit, I soon coaxed the Green Weenie to a shuddering stop in fourth gear in front of Mary Sue's house.

Mary Sue, the amiable daughter of a small-town barber, came from a world even more provincial than my own. With her beatific smile and even temper, she was the perfect traveling companion, always up for whatever came along. I had various stopovers planned along the way—with my brother Paul in the mountains west of Denver; my great-aunts Sophie Bauer in Salt

Lake City and Marie Lloyd in San Francisco. That was fine with
Mary Sue. Though we had spoken vaguely of Seattle, I wasn't
even sure what our final destination would be. That was fine, too.
We could talk about anything and everything—or, for endless
miles, nothing at all. One subject, however, got almost no mention: the "time I died." As the days went by, the episode lodged
deeper and deeper into the recesses of my memory, like the little
lump that was Toto, burrowed in his bed of shredded newspaper.
Better to let sleeping hamsters lie, too.

Besides, it just wasn't that easy to discuss it. When we stayed
with Paul, at his cabin near the timberline at Berthoud Pass,
Colorado, I thought it would be a good time and place for a heart-
to-heart talk with my talented little brother, whom I still called
Pinky, his childhood nickname. Pinky could see I had changed—
his conservative, straitlaced big sister was looking more and more
like a hippie chick. By contrast, Pinky seemed like the same way-
ward rock-and-roll songwriter he'd always been, with his long red
hair, his music, his pack of Irish setter puppies gamboling at his
feet. But Pinky was also changing. Up in the Rocky Mountains,
he had given up drugs and become a born-again Christian. He
was writing songs in a new genre which would bring him world-
wide recognition as Paul Clark, one of the founders of contemporary Christian music. Pinky was just beginning his trip, and so
was I. It was still too early for the travelogues.

As Mary Sue and I continued our westward journey over the
mountain ranges, I became uncharacteristically confident of my
driving prowess. Descending from the switchbacks of the Wa-
satch Mountains into the Salt Lake Valley, I announced to Mary
Sue that I was Mario Andretti. I stuck my head out the window
and screeched in perfect emulation of tires burning rubber on the
hairpin turns. The wind whipped my face as we went faster and
faster; I was fearless. I felt completely indestructible as I steered

the Green Weenie within feet of sheer mountain cliffs, oblivious
to and unconcerned with the danger.

I knew we were safe because the presence that had abided
with me since I blubbered my way across Kansas was very much
along for the joyride. And it truly was a joyride—I wasn't experiencing the thrill of danger but the thrill of being fully alive. I
felt so totally protected that nothing seemed risky. "Ha, ha," I
laughed maniacally. "This is great!"

One look at Mary Sue, however, told me she was in a different
frame of mind. She still wore her beatific smile, but her eyes had
widened to Little Orphan Annie orbs and her long brown hair
was flying straight back, as if frozen in a gale. As for poor little
Toto, he'd tucked himself into a ball and was rolling harmlessly
around in his cage as we careened around each turn. His fur was
standing completely on end, like a tiny fluffy hedgehog. I finally
took pity on him and eased up on the speed.

After a few days in Salt Lake City, with Aunt Sophie, we
continued West. Driving the Green Weenie across the Utah desert, I began to get that I'm-not-really-driving-this-car feeling
again. There was hardly any traffic on the road, so I decided to
test this strange perception. *Look ma, no hands.* Keeping my foot
on the accelerator because I lacked *total* faith, I turned away from
the steering wheel and rummaged for sandwich makings in the
grocery bag behind Mary Sue's seat. Using both hands, I un-
wrapped a loaf of white bread, took two slices, and carefully
twisted the wrapper tight again. I found two new jars of peanut
butter and jelly and handed them to Mary Sue. Then I fished
around for a knife while my incredibly accommodating companion opened the jars and held them for me. She seemed unfazed
as I dipped into first the peanut butter, then the jelly, and smeared
them on the bread without so much as a glance at the road.

"Do you fully realize that no one is driving the car?"

"Yes," she said calmly.

I put down the knife and poked her hard in the arm with my finger. "Hey," she said, her voice rising in a rare protest.

"I just wanted to check if you were real. How come you're so easy about going along for the ride?" I asked, somewhat suspicious of her reality, for the line between reality and unreality was becoming blurry.

"Because I *am* along for the ride," she replied, as if the reason were so obvious she need not elaborate further.

I tore the sandwich in two and gave her half. Settling back into my seat, I munched my sandwich in bemused silence as the Green Weenie hurtled toward Nevada. Mary Sue did the same. Toto snoozed in his cage. What a crew we made. *All of us* were along for the ride. Metaphorically at least, we were astonishingly content to leave the driving to—well, we didn't exactly know who, but it sure wasn't Greyhound. As I polished off the last of the sandwich, I shot Mary Sue a sidewise glance. I would not have been surprised if the real Mary Sue Bollig was still back in Hays, Kansas, and an angel that looked, sounded, and acted like Mary Sue had climbed into the car to accompany me on a trip I never would have made by myself. A tiny giggle escaped her Mona Lisa lips but not a word of admonition. Her trust (in me? the Green Weenie's marvelous alignment? our invisible driver?) was astounding. Still eying her skeptically, I finished my meal and resumed control of the wheel. The reality test was over. Reality lost.

Ah, San Francisco. During the summer of 1970, there were few places in the Western Hemisphere more cool or more happening than the Haight-Ashbury district in San Francisco, where my great-aunt Marie had made arrangements for us to stay in a young friend's apartment. As we unpacked the car in front of the bay-windowed building, I could not take my eyes off the street sign. Haight Street, *the Haight Street,* in *the* Haight-Ashbury District, in the hippie capital of the world. I mused how ironic it was that the center of the universe for the Love Generation was a street named Haight.

I loved San Francisco. Mary Sue and I belonged there, belonged with the other bell-bottomed and beaded kids with no permanent address and no one to whom we had to report. Such exhilarating freedom we felt as we strolled street after famous street, so far from Kansas. Neither one of us had taken serious stock of the change in our appearances since our journey began, but now we looked like we had been someplace with stories to tell. Tan, slightly weathered, Mary Sue and I wore identical brushed leather, floppy brimmed hats, she over long brown braids, me over loose blond pigtails. Tourists took our pictures. We were hippies.

The trouble with the Haight was it was a little *too* happening. Everywhere we went, we saw posters advertising the Rolling Stones' upcoming free concert at Altamount, the disastrous event that foretold the beginning of the end of the Age of Aquarius. Bad drugs, bad vibes, bad folks—as exemplified by the Hell's Angels thugs who "kept order" at Altamount—all were converging on San Francisco, the country's phantasmagoric ground zero. We were lucky to be there while it was still magical, and get out before things got ugly.

Before long, we were on the road again, zooming north on Interstate 5 as if we already knew the way. The more miles I put under the tires of the Green Weenie, the more energized I became. No more lollygagging and sightseeing now; we stopped only to put gas in the car and drove on. Portland, Olympia, Tacoma—they flew by in a blur. As we topped the long rise south of Seattle near Boeing Field, we watched the city unfold before us like a beautiful tapestry. We saw snowy mountains to the east and west;

giant container ships jammed along the busy waterfront; darkly forested peninsulas and islands stretching across the silvery waters of Puget Sound.

It was a picture-perfect layout. Except, that is, for an enormous billboard that suddenly came into view with the jarring message: WILL THE LAST PERSON LEAVING SEATTLE PLEASE TURN OUT THE LIGHTS? Unbeknown to us on our carefree meanderings from deepest Kansas, our arrival in Seattle coincided with the worst recession in the city's history. The downturn was triggered by huge layoffs at Boeing, the aerospace company which at the time was responsible for one out of every five jobs in the region; it would take years for the city to recover. But that didn't matter to me, because I had plenty of time. This was where I was going to live, work, make friends, fall in love, marry, have children, grow old, and die. I knew it, with the same certainty that I realized I had to leave Leawood. "We're not in Kansas anymore, Toto," I announced to my companions.

To myself I said simply, "Homey home."

CHAPTER FOUR

DANCE
WITH THE DEMON

▼

THE HOUSE WAS INVISIBLE from the street, as invisible as the loathsome energy that emanated from it. The old, white, two-story farmhouse sat at the farthest reaches of a long, treeless lot choked with weeds and blackberry bushes. Most of the lower windows were broken or missing. Undisturbed dust on the sills and jagged glass said that not even vagrants had recently sought refuge inside.

I stepped across the rotting wood porch. The knob on the front door turned easily. Air currents created by the opening door sent wafts of dust billowing around the living room. In the afternoon sunlight streaming through a picture window, the dust looked like snow.

I surveyed this space, as well as the adjoining dining room, before moving into the kitchen. Spider webs were oddly absent despite the house's disuse. The house was simply barren of any form of life. In fact, it felt like a very long time, if ever, since laughter or love had echoed through the structure.

"Homey home?" I tentatively asked the house. Silence. I liked that in a house.

In the two years since I had arrived in Seattle I had mainly lived in cheap apartments. Now I had a chance to live in a real house for the first time since I left home to go to college. My own house! In exchange for my efforts to create a livable environment, the landlord promised to make repairs, pay for utilities, and never raise the $125-a-month rent. The deal was just too good to pass up.

During the next two years I poured a considerable amount of time and labor into refurbishing the house and yard. The walls and carpeting were redone in warm, cheerful colors. I planted grass, put in a garden, burned back the blackberry bushes, and worked to convert the house and grounds into a charming setting. And after two years of toil, the results were . . . okay.

Grass plugs and garden plants withered. Hardy houseplants carefully tended indoors died or grew in a sickly fashion. No touch of warmth or whimsy got much of a foothold. The house seemed to suck up all the energy my roommate and I put into it, and gave back nothing in return. The milieu of funky old furniture and knickknacks that filled the rooms failed to add the atmosphere of warmth I tried to establish. It was the sapping, enervating essence of the environment that made the house disturbing.

In 1974, I officially threw my teaching plans out the window when I entered the Graduate School of Social Work at the University of Washington, intending to specialize in the field of child abuse. My days were spent in classes and as a social-work cadet with the Tacoma Head Start program. In the evenings, I worked on my thesis, sold Avon products, and indulged my new passion—belly dancing—with a local folk-dancing ensemble. My blond hair and fairskinned midwestern looks didn't exactly jibe with my middle-eastern stage name, Kahlila a wadi Kadeeshi, or my exotic hip-hugging costume, which shimmered with hundreds of dangling Lebanese metal coins.

On my infrequent visits with my parents I sometimes broached the subject of "when I died" with my father. What I gleaned in those brief exchanges I stored zealously away, constructing a disjointed narrative with bits and pieces from his memory and mine. I knew that my sudden collapse at the Department of Motor Vehicles had caused a chaotic scene, and that some people had actually become irritated because my body blocked both the entrance and exit to the office. I must have been an arresting sight: The skin around my mouth turned a ghoulish hue due to oxygen deprivation, and the misconnected ventilator forced air under my skin—a condition known as epithelial emphysema—causing me to resemble "an inflated balloon," according to my father.

But these were all surface observations, recollections from "topside." I never dealt with the content of my other memories—the lingering impressions of an experience that transcended time, space, language, and, of course, my own body. Like tunes that stubbornly float in our heads when we wish they would go away, these insistent images clung to my subconscious. The light, the particulate fog, the sight of my lifeless body in profile on the pavement. Yet when I tried to examine what they meant, they slipped away. It was as if I could hear the chorus but not the melody, fragments of song but not enough to "name that tune." Frustrated, I gave up trying to understand these snippets of memory—just as I gave up talking to my father about it.

What I could not avoid noticing, however, was how guided I felt when it came to jobs. I began to joke about how finding satisfying work was like living on the automatic door opener of a grocery store. I seemed always to be standing in the right place at the right time for the doors to open. The two occasions when I deliberately went against the grain of my instincts proved ridiculous and insulting.

The first time I ignored the screaming NO inside my head was when I interviewed for a job as a health club employee. The male interviewer asked me to raise my skirt, presumably so he could determine if I had a firm enough bottom to be a good physical model of the success of their program. Appalled at his lechery, I wanted to storm out of his office. But it was the time of the big Boeing bust in Seattle, and I was competing for work, any work, with over 100,000 unemployed people. I was hungry. I complied with his indecent proposal and got the position of trainer and nutrition consultant. I, who never walked when I could drive and thought peanut M&Ms were better nutrition than those with chocolate centers, quit the following day after refusing to wear the revealing Roman toga and five-inch spike heels I was given as a uniform.

The second time I ignored the feeling that I was heading in entirely the wrong direction was when I paid a business progressively named The Women's Employment Agency to find me a job. I was told to return to take a short test, which I assumed would be an interest/experience/education survey. It was a typing test. When I politely informed the tester that I didn't know how to type and never planned to learn, I was told that placement depended entirely on the typing test—five minutes in the center of a room with another applicant banging out her test on speed and accuracy while waiting women lined the walls and watched. Amused, I spent my five minutes slowly pecking out letters with two index fingers while the woman next to me whirred away at a speed of about nine hundred words a minute without chipping a long painted nail or losing the jack-o'-lantern grin that dominated the lower two-thirds of her face. I never got placed.

The job I got that I really loved began by following a hunch to explore my neighborhood. What I found was Ryther Child Center, where I applied for an open receptionist position. Ironically, the application "accidentally" got routed to the director of child care instead, and she hired me for a position I didn't expect but was entirely suited for. I became an on-site house mom for twenty-two emotionally disturbed children and adolescents.

This job became the springboard to my career in social work. Most of the kids were throwaways, the flotsam and jetsam of uncaring adult relationships, and they were starved for affection. They got plenty of it from me, dipping into a reservoir of unconditional love and compassion I didn't even know I had. When they acted out, I was surprised at how easy it was to put myself in their place and empathize with these damaged, traumatized youngsters. Me, a child of privilege who'd been assiduously sheltered from anything that resembled hard knocks. This talent for caring, if you could call it that, began to appear after I nearly died.

Fixing, cleaning, and painting had begun on the lower floor of my house. The last area upstairs to get painted was the walk-in closet of my bedroom. The bedroom itself was spacious and light—it even had a territorial view. The closet was horrid. I couldn't pinpoint exactly why I procrastinated about giving it a new coat of paint, except that whenever I entered it, I felt dreadful.

Full of resolve one Saturday afternoon, I stepped inside the closet with a gallon of white paint and a brush. Immediately my attention was drawn to a large stain on the wall at the far end. I froze, almost literally, and backed out. I had felt a decided chill. Shaking it off, I stepped back inside the closet. "Yuk," I said aloud, and darted right out again. What was I afraid of? A stain? Absurd. I dashed back into the closet, attacking the fearful thing kamikaze style with brush and paint. At once the chilly feeling stopped. No spot, no scare. I made quick work of the rest of the job.

When I returned the next day to check my handiwork, I got an unpleasant surprise. The spot was back, oozing with a vileness that made my heart pound and froze my feet to the floor. Like a diver who's spent too much time underwater, I gasped for air as I burst from the closet and ran down the stairs. Rather than acknowledge the existence of anything paranormal, I decided that it was an attack of claustrophobia. The idea that I literally had an anxiety closet made me laugh and removed the last vestiges of tension I felt. More determined than ever to banish the spot, I dashed back into the closet. The stain reeked with such a sinister quality that I was afraid my shaking hand would not hold the brush as I painted over it again.

Again the splotch returned. I called for reinforcements. A friend of mine visited, checked out the closet and told me not to worry. "It's just a bad spot. All you need . . . ," and he chatted on and on about the advantages of oil-based, high-gloss enamel paint for this kind of situation. I wasn't to worry my pretty little head over it, he told me. He'd handle the problem himself from here on out.

My friend displayed increasing fatigue and listlessness over the next several days, as he repeatedly told me that the stain had returned. It bled through seven coats of enamel paint before he gave up, utterly demoralized. Meanwhile, the stain continued to ooze, in all its mocking glory. It seemed to have a life of its own. I thought about how empty and dead the house felt before I moved in. Maybe it hadn't been lifeless, but dormant—and human habitation had awakened its malign energy. Maybe the stain was a warning, some sign from the netherworld.

Nah. This wasn't a late-night TV horror show; this was reality, and in reality there was no such thing as The Blob. Finally,
I did what I should have done in the first place—called the landlord and told him to send over a carpenter with a piece of plywood
and some nails. Once the stain was boarded up and storage boxes
were piled in front of it, I never gave it a second thought. No
spot was going to keep me from inhabiting the deal of the century.

A few months later, I had friends over for dinner when the dining
room lights began to go off and on. They didn't flicker, but actually turned completely off, briefly plunging the room into darkness before turning back on. After a few minutes of this on-again,
off-again pattern, the kitchen and living room lights joined in,
while guests and I grew uneasy.

Part of me briefly wondered if I wasn't somehow responsible
for the light show. Ever since "when I died," I'd noticed that
under certain emotional circumstances, street lights blinked off
as I drove underneath them. The effect was particularly notice-
able when I was driving fast on a highway. I could observe the
lights going out overhead—ping, ping, ping in rapid succession—
then watch in my rearview mirror as they slowly returned to normal in the distance. This was no parlor trick; I could never predict
when it would happen except that most often it was when I was
feeling emotionally high with happiness. But I wasn't feeling that
way at the dinner table, and now the lights in the house were
flashing on and off, downstairs and up, like a pinball machine.

My two friends and I stood in the center of the living room
as all of the lights suddenly doused. "Probably a fuse," noted one
guest. Then all of the lights returned. "Probably a transformer,"
said the same guest. Then the lights went out. On the way to a
flashlight the lights went on, off, on, off, faster and faster until

the pace reached the throbbing frenzy of a strobe light. My other guest, who had run upstairs to check on the electrical status of the second floor, yelled down that the lights were behaving the same way up there, too. Suddenly the pattern changed. Now lights went off and on in the living room only, then the dining room, then all of the rooms until what before had been a rhythmic and increasingly faster off-on pattern throughout the house became an erratic one. The tempo of randomly darkened and lit rooms continued to a fever pitch. Then all at once it came to a stop, as if the music the lights had been dancing to had come to an end. My guests and I were nervous and confused, and we abandoned the house en masse. I spent the night elsewhere, too intimidated by the bizarre light show to stay there alone.

By the next day I rationalized that loose wires had undoubtedly caused the previous night's disturbance. Or perhaps a mouse or a squirrel, temporarily stuck in a wall at a spot where several wires crossed, interrupted electrical flow as it struggled to get free. Hoping that in addition to everything else I didn't have a fried squirrel rotting between walls, I called the landlord, who sent out an electrician. He found nothing amiss, but was curious about my assertion that the lights had gone haywire both upstairs and downstairs. That would be next to impossible, he said, since each floor had its own electrical feed and was wired separately into its own fuse box.

Uneventful weeks passed. I returned home from an evening out and flopped on the couch with the newspaper in hand. Immediately lights on the entire lower floor began the same accelerated, random pattern of going off and on. There was no warning, no gradual increase in speed, just BOOM—instant amusement park. I threw down the paper and tore across the house to the bottom of the stairs where I had earlier tossed my purse and car keys. From this vantage point I could see the same rapid flashing of lights in the upstairs rooms as well. In fear and confusion I ran from the house and jumped into the car. Backing out of the driveway, every window of the house winked at me as the lights continued to behave as if mischievous children were dashing from room to room playing some macabre game.

I drove to the nearby house of an acquaintance who was a police officer. Sorely tempted to ask him to go over and shoot my house, I asked instead to use his phone and called the emergency service number for the electric company. In less than an hour, the cop and I met the electric company representative at my house, where the lights, of course, were behaving in a perfectly civilized manner. The utility man did a full inside and outside assessment of the electric system and changed every fuse in both boxes before suggesting that the old house be rewired. He couldn't account for the situation I described, but at least to my face he didn't write me off as a kook.

I got a roommate. My thinking was that either I would be less likely to imagine the house was stirring with increased unexplained activity or that the house itself would not misbehave in the presence of another tenant.

Normalcy reigned for a few months until one night, after returning from a late movie, I found a note from my new roommate stuck to the door. In the illumination from the porch light I read, "Don't go in the house. I think someone's inside. Call me." She left a phone number and the time when she had scribbled this message. It was written less than half an hour earlier. She probably had heard a noise and jumped to conclusions, I surmised as I entered the dark house.

Before I was able to cross the room to turn on a light I saw it. Coming from the direction of the hallway was a swirling mist, approximately waist level, incandescent in a color resembling hot magenta. Even though it softly illuminated the living room, its glow carried a dark quality. Perhaps because I didn't believe my eyes I ran for the phone instead of the door. I called my neighbor the cop. In the amount of time it took to dial his number and listen to a few rings, the magenta mist had expanded to fill the dining room and what I could see of the kitchen with red-violet light. At last the cop answered his phone. What words I used to describe the scene closing in on me sounded like gibberish to my ear. The cop said, "Drop the phone. Get out of the house. Now!" I ran.

Like a dreadful nightmare it seemed I could not move my legs fast enough. One step ahead of the grasp of the mist I got out of the house and into the car. Cursing my hands for their shaking, I struggled to get the key into the ignition. The car squealed out of the driveway.

Later I called my roommate and told her that the police were called in. My roommate moved out.

Friends recommended that I move, but I couldn't afford not to stay. I'd invested a tremendous amount of time and effort in the place, and I was so poor that I believed any place I could afford on my part-time salary from the University of Washington would be a worse dump.

It was late summer. Out-of-town guests came and went. I barbecued outside on my hibachi, sunbathed, mowed the weeds. The usual. One night, quite late because it was already dark, I decided to go to a party at a friend's house. I was applying makeup in the mirror of the upstairs bathroom when something strange caught my attention. The lights were out in both the hallway and my bedroom. Ever since my roommate moved out, I had kept the house ablaze with lights. I rationalized this behavior by telling myself I could thus easily spot the big spiders that normally crawled inside this time of year. The normal world of crab-size spiders was scary enough as it was. I didn't want to admit that there really might be a paranormal world to be scared of as well. Filled with dread that the house might turn into a bewitched light show again, I further realized I was only wearing a bra and underpants. "Oh, great," I thought to myself. "Where in that dark bedroom are my clothes? And my purse? And where did I drop the car keys?"

I was just about to leave the only lit room—in the whole house for all I knew—when I heard a loud metallic sound. I paused at the bathroom sink, unsure I had heard anything at all. Then I heard it again, the very loud sound of metal slowly being pulled against metal, the sound an anchor chain would make as it was slowly pulled over a ship's railing. Clank, clank, clank, clank. The grating noise continued to get louder, loud enough that I could identify the area from where it seemed to originate. It was coming from the useless room at the end of the hall that I never did get around to fixing up. That useless room where one houseguest's bath towels had turned disgustingly sour in only two days.

The long, drawn-out clanking got louder, as if an amplification system was being turned up one notch at a time. That was it for me. I was out of there, clothes or no clothes.

I quickened my pace to the bathroom door. I never made it across the threshold. Something that felt like an invisible arm hit me across the chest, or rather, I ran into an invisible arm with such force that it sent me reeling backward. It had such an arm-like feeling—room temperature, soft on the outside with a harder core—that I turned to see who had blocked my way even though I knew I was alone in the bathroom.

I couldn't catch my breath. I couldn't scream. I could only stare into the empty space in the doorway from which I had just been barred. The clanking sound grew deafening. In pure animal panic I put my hands over my ears, shut my eyes tight, and stumbled backward. I hit a little table by the bathtub that held magazines and books. It crashed to the floor. I kept falling back until I fell into my big, claw-footed bathtub. I was completely paralyzed with fear.

I panted in asthmatic fashion and stared at the darkness on the other side of the door. The clanking leveled off at an ear-shattering decibel level, then suddenly stopped. The silence seemed as loud as the sound of the huge chain. Then just as suddenly it started again, but this time the clanking was moving. Even though the sound was not growing louder, I could hear it getting closer. It moved down the hall toward the bathroom in a slow, methodical, menacing cadence. Whatever was creating the sound knew exactly where I was. I sensed that if I didn't go out and investigate it, it was going to come in and investigate me. My thoughts went on hold.

The sound moved closer and closer. It was torturing and taunting me with the slowness of its approach. I felt completely trapped, unable even to use my voice to protect myself. But then, above the din of the ever-nearing clanking, I found my voice and used it to its best purpose.

"God help me!" I wailed, drawing out each word as if I'd never hear the sound of my voice again.

In moments I was awash with an incredible peace and a sense of loving support. I knew at once that I was not alone in the bathroom, had never been alone in the bathroom or anywhere else. A presence I could not see with my eyes spoke to my heart with the knowledge that whatever was coming down the hall was coming specifically for me, but I was completely protected. I knew that the invisible arm at the doorway, belonging to this presence perhaps, was standing guard over me. I felt awash again, this time in awareness. I knew I must not leave the bathroom. For some reason, at that particular time the bathroom, with its lights burning brighter than I had seen before, was a safe haven.

In what I sensed was rage, the clanking grew in volume, louder than I thought I could tolerate. I began to lose trust in the presence, in the safety of the room, in my prayer. "Run!" screamed the voice of doubt and fear in my head. "Run!" Whatever was making the ear-splitting sound had not quite rounded the end of the hallway by the bathroom door. If I was going to bolt it had to be right then. "Run!"

I pulled myself shakily to a standing position, then fell right back into the tub at what I next saw. In the open doorway separating the bathroom from the hall appeared a filmlike substance, like a desert mirage, there but not there. The darkness behind the door seemed distorted, as if I were viewing it through heat vapors.

The door was sealed. A great sense of peace and protection again filled room. Actually it never left the room. Only my faith had gone.

The clanking ceased. The darkness on the other side remained. So did the "vaporlock," as I came to call it.

I yanked a bath towel off the rack and pulled it over me like a blanket. Never taking my eyes off the doorway, I curled up in the tub, my hands in a position of prayer between my head and the porcelain surface.

I awakened to the sight of early morning sunlight streaming through my bedroom window across the hall. A warm summer breeze gently moved the curtains.

How could I have fallen into the tub and gone to sleep? I stiffly pulled myself up and stepped out toward the door. Then I remembered. The door, the chains, the darkness. "Wow, that was sure a doozy of a nightmare," I mumbled sleepily as I fell into my own comfy bed. No more dreams disturbed my sleep that day.

Was it a hallucination? A nightmare? Ever since my dying experience in Shawnee Mission, I was prone to sudden sleep attacks; conceivably I might have sat on the edge of the tub, conked out, and had a bad dream. I sought answers from a doctor, who examined me and diagnosed my condition as narcolepsy—a nervous-system disorder characterized by periodic, uncontrollable episodes of deep sleep. As for my "nightmare," I convinced myself that it was a hypnogogic hallucination, typical of narcoleptics— a dream so vivid that it can be construed as being real. The doctor prescribed a small daily dose of Ritalin, a medication often used to control both narcolepsy and hyperactivity.

I took the pills, but they didn't end the experiences I was having in the house. In fact, as time wore on, they intensified and became even more real.

Laurie Gates, a classmate from graduate school, became my next housemate. We were perfectly compatible. Not only did we share the same academic interests and lifestyles, but Laurie brought culinary skills to the household, adding a repertoire of recipes to my own can-opener style of cooking.

Laurie was out for the evening, so it was with surprise that I heard a female voice call out my name from the top of the stairs. Before I could figure out how someone had entered the house, my name was called again.

"Kim?" I heard in a voice that sounded like my sister's.

"Kristy? Kristy, is that you?" I asked in utter astonishment.

My younger sister, Kristy, was living with her husband, Randy, in Shawnee Mission. Why on earth would she be here? Payback, maybe. A few years earlier I had pulled a similar stunt by showing up unannounced in her room at Kansas State University.

My conjecturing came to an abrupt end as Kristy stepped just outside my bedroom doorway. I was too flabbergasted to move. Kristy was my favorite person on earth. We had shared the same canopy bed most of our lives and had never exchanged a disagreeable word.

"Hi, sis!" she said in her customary perky manner.

I watched all four foot eleven of her step into the doorway. There she was just as I had last seen her—towhead blond, short hair, attired in her favorite navy-blue dress, her demure smile belying her wiseacre personality. It was every bit my sister, with one exception—her eyes. They were black, not hazel. Completely black. I could see no pupil, no cornea, no iris, nor the whites of her eyes. I stared into pure and utter darkness.

Confusion and fear reached out for me as the image of my sister took a step closer. My capacity to think clearly came to an abrupt end as I gaped at something that looked, sounded, and acted like Kristy, but most certainly wasn't.

As if knowing that the jig was up, the Kristy clone, still smiling at me, stepped backward onto the landing at the top of the stairs and out of my sight. Everything had happened so fast that I still could not register the entirety of the events. With a love for my sister greater than my fear of the eyes I had just beheld, I bounded across the room to where she had stood.

"Kristy?" I called out, "Kristy?"

No response.

I dashed downstairs still calling her name, in the increasingly unlikely event that it was really my sister. Then I saw the position of the button on the front-door knob. The door was locked from the inside.

The room took a dizzy dive as my brain tried to formulate a rational conclusion about what had transpired. Could I have somehow fallen asleep, just for a moment? I knew one thing for sure, though. There was something familiar about what had happened, real or not. What emanated from the Kristy clone's eyes held the same diabolic essence as whatever terrorized me on the night of the really bad "dream" in the bathroom.

Surprise visitations by something demonic in human form happened to me more than once. After appearing as Kristy, this threatening force, being, or whatever term you wish to use to describe it, appeared as a longtime friend of mine named Jim, and later as a new acquaintance of mine named Jon.

These visits were brief but terrifying, largely because of how helpless they made me feel. It was as if I were being stalked by an intruder who came and went at will, who was toying with me. Its motive wasn't to hurt me, exactly, but to overpower me—to possess me. Demonic possession, what nonsense. I couldn't believe that I was even entertaining the notion. But how else to explain what I knew in my heart, that a negative force had as its goal gaining control of my nascent spirituality—my soul?

I was particularly vulnerable to these experiences when my physical or emotional strength was at a low ebb. In late 1976—just a few months before meeting Maria—I had returned to Leawood to recuperate from surgery for an intestinal abscess. My recovery was slow; I was weak and depressed. I was beginning, finally, to feel the sting of being different from other people, and the strain and loneliness of leading two separate lives. There was my "topside" life as a highly competent social worker with an address book full of friends and a "no problem, I can handle this" attitude. Then there was the other Kim, who harbored unsettling, not to mention inexplicable memories of "nearly dying" and fears of being stalked by a demon. I couldn't discuss these things with anyone I knew. Hey, I was supposed to take care of nutcases. I wasn't supposed to be one myself.

One day as I languished on the couch in the family room of my parents' house, I felt particularly low. Life seemed so hard and so wearisome; I wished everything would just stop. I was trapped on an endless merry-go-round and I wanted off. I wanted to let go. That was it: Just . . . let . . . go. I thought about this as I lay on the couch, more tired and empty of spirit than I had a right to be. I was not yet thirty years old.

Sunlight poured in through the French doors in the entry hall, reflecting off the polished, white wood floors. Lethargically, I stared at the pattern of light, and that was when I saw him— it—again.

The figure of a man stepped soundlessly into the light. Because of the glare, his face was difficult to make out, but I could tell he was strikingly beautiful, his dark hair combed slickly back. He wore an elegant dark suit. His eyes were also dark, liquid, empty—incapable of human response. The familiar helplessness and fear kept me rooted to the spot as he took a step toward me. Then another. Slowly, like a hunter approaching his prey. No need to hurry; I wasn't going anywhere.

Almost as slowly, awareness penetrated my terror. This—this thing wanted to seize me, possess me. I was the prey. Prey? Pray.

Pray! That was it—I needed to pray, and pray loudly, right now! But what to pray? How to pray? As the demon loomed closer, my thoughts were a jumble. I couldn't think. Then the words to an old church hymn came to mind—one my Grandma Tyra loved to sing.

"I know that my Redeemer lives . . ." I croaked, barely above a whisper.

The thing stopped in its tracks, just like that. I sang out the words, more boldly now: "I know that my Redeemer lives!" The demon glared at me with those awful eyes and held his ground. Frantically I tried to remember the rest of the hymn, but it was no good. Fear crushed me; I couldn't breathe; I couldn't think. My mind went blank again, leaving me weak with dread.

But the prayer that had taken shape in my heart had been heard by a loving God. I suddenly sensed the presence of a mass of beings around me, visible yet invisible. Though I couldn't exactly see them, I could sense their movement and could feel their energy. They exuded a holiness that filled every inch of space in the room, forming a phalanx of spiritual defenders between me and the demon. I knew without being told that I was in the presence of angels. They were putting on a show of force—holy force—and there was no question their side would win.

The loathsome visitor retreated backward across the room, staring at me the whole time, his glare defiant and spiteful. His wordless message was directed not to my guardians but to me, and I understood its meaning as clearly as if he had shouted it out loud.

"You are mine. If not now, later. I'm always here, always watching." With that, he pushed through the crowd of holy spirits and I watched him disappear. He seemed to break into millions of little pieces, like a cloud of splattered black paint suspended in the air. Then everything—the dark cloud and the angelic beings—disappeared and I found myself staring once again at the shaft of sunlight spreading across the floor.

I was struck dumb. My mind struggled to grasp the information presented by the drama that had just unfolded. The demon stalker was certainly not confined to my house in Seattle or to any one place, I realized now with horror. Was he right? Was there no escape? But the hymn and the mention of my Redeemer had certainly stopped him in his tracks. And was he really a human male in true form or was that a guise, like his earliest appearances? And his eyes. Why did his eyes remain unchanged even though he could obviously alter the rest of his appearance? And what in heaven's name got between us? Angels, I knew it somehow. But an army of angels?

What in the world had happened here? Perhaps it had all been a figment of my fevered imagination or my short-circuited, narcoleptic brain? Had I fallen rapidly and without warning into a deep sleep? Maybe it had been a hypnogogic hallucination. No one knew the signs better than I; thanks to my regular research at the University of Washington School of Medicine library, I had become something of a self-taught expert on everything written about this obscure syndrome.

But certain characteristics of my experiences—for instance, the repeated appearance of the same character in a sort of continuing narrative—didn't correspond to what I read was supposed to happen in the medical literature. And it didn't correlate to my growing conviction that there was something real there, something true, something that defied all attempts at a rational explanation, despite my numerous trips to the library. When I got right down to it, I wasn't sure what constituted "real" anyway. Was my "topside" life more real than these demonic experiences, and my memories of a life beyond this one? Or was it the other way around?

Why was this happening to me? Why the demon, why the angels, why the challenge to my sense of what was "real"? The answers, I felt, would be found in my job as a social worker counseling the dying. I knew I was good at helping people in crisis, in life-and-death situations, and that I was powerfully attracted to this work. I knew also that it had much to teach me and I had much to learn. But I was still hazy on the specifics.

There are people who have prophetic, global visions which foresee cataclysmic events, such as the eruption of Mount St. Helen's. Sometimes they're right, sometimes not. My visions have always been on a much smaller, more personal scale—the demon being a prime example. And I have to admit that their accuracy rate is less than perfect. Nearly a year before it actually happened, I had a dream that correctly foretold the setting and occasion when I would meet my future husband. But I was dead wrong, so to speak, with a vision that predicted my death in the crash of a white plane before my thirty-fifth birthday. I always pay close attention to these messages from my spiritual consciousness. But I put great stock in my—everyone's—ability to exercise free will. That's one of many variables that play havoc with the most explicit prognostications.

I was just beginning to formulate these ideas at the time of my encounter with the demonic figure in Kansas. There would be other encounters with dark forces, and with angels, too. I was increasingly certain that just as my near-death experience had awakened in me a positive energy I never knew I had, so it made me susceptible to negative energy as well.

I do not now have, nor have I ever had any interest in the occult or psychic phenomena. I pay no attention to Satan-mongerers or soothsayers. But I recognize that there are negative forces as well as positive ones at work in the world, and for those of us who may be more vulnerable than most, it's prudent to avoid certain situations or settings in which negativity can flourish. If you're bothered by alcohol, you stay out of bars. In my case, I don't mess with Ouija boards, Tarot cards, mediums, and the like; to respect my own psychic energy, I try to stay grounded in the here and now.

There are few places closer to the here-and-now than Harborview Medical Center. That was where I belonged, where I was sure my destiny would be found, where the explanations for these experiences might lie. It was time to haul myself up off the couch and get on with it. So that's exactly what I did, and within a few weeks recovered my strength sufficiently to return to Seattle.

Five months later, I was on duty at the hospital when I was summoned to the bedside of an agitated patient in the coronary care unit. Her name was Maria, and she had a strange story to tell me—something about a shoe. As the trajectories of our separate lives intersected, my mission snapped into crystalline focus. There would be many more Marias and many more stories, and I would be called to hear them. It would be my ministry, my service, my joy. I would offer comfort not only to those who were sick or dying, but those who were recovering or grieving. To all of them I carried a simple message, one that human beings have sought since the earliest times: You are not alone. You will never be alone.

It was a message that I finally understood myself.

CHAPTER FIVE

AWAKENINGS

▼

P ENNY BYERS was a sad case. Even staff members inured to
tragedy said so. Only seventeen years old, she was admitted
to intensive care following a suicide attempt. Usually, kids
her age were sent to Children's Hospital and Medical Center at
the University of Washington, but the medics brought her to
Harborview because it was the closest medical facility to her
home, and thus the one with the best chance of saving the life
she tried to throw away.

Night and day, Penny's mother sat by her unconscious daughter's bedside in the MICU (medical intensive care unit), telling
anyone who would listen how she had left work in the middle of
that fateful day and raced home because her intuition told her
something was wrong. Something was. Penny had skipped school
and taken an overdose of black-market barbiturates in response
to a soured romance and overwhelming adolescent angst. Her
mother found her comatose and near death.

Eventually, Penny regained consciousness and pulled
through, but it was several days before all her organs were func-
tioning again. When she was able to talk, I visited her and asked
the same questions I had begun asking all my patients who'd had
a close brush with death. What was your last memory before los-

ing consciousness? Do you remember anything after that? Usually, this line of inquiry elicited quizzical looks or blank stares; in the eight weeks since the Maria episode, I'd yet to hear anyone else tell me of a genuine near-death experience. Penny was different.

Right off the bat, Penny told me that she remembered wanting to die before blacking out from her overdose, but that after going to a "gray place," her "Oompah" sent her back. "What?" I practically shouted, leaping to my feet from the stool next to her bed. Had I heard right?

Penny thought I was confused by the reference to *Oompah*. She explained it was her nickname for her grandfather, which she had bestowed on him when she was a small child unable to pronounce *Grandpa*.

"Where's Oompah now?" I asked.

"He's dead," Penny said. In fact, she had hardly known him—he'd died fifteen years earlier. But she never forgot the love and attention he showed her, and she recognized him immediately in the "gray place."

"Look," I said, "before you tell me more, I want you to know that what happened to you was real." I had carefully rehearsed these words for the day I knew would come, when a patient would describe an experience similar to Maria's and mine. My hope was to reassure patients who might be afraid to relate an experience they thought sounded bizarre or crazy. Penny needed no such reassurance.

"I know," she said calmly. "It was more real than this." She glanced around her room. She was composed and speaking normally, without the flat affect commonly seen in people who are deeply depressed. I asked her to tell me more about what she remembered after she had overdosed.

Penny said she found herself walking in a place where everything seemed gray. She didn't recognize the location, and couldn't tell if it was indoors or outdoors. Suddenly, Oompah appeared and blocked her way. He looked more like a young man than the elderly grandfather she'd known, and she was elated to be with him again. He picked her up in his arms and carried her to a rocking chair. There he sat, with Penny on his lap, and proceeded to admonish her for trying to take her life.

"Penny, what have you done?" he asked sternly. "This is not your time. You have to go back. It's not your time." Penny felt such peace and comfort in his lap that she begged to be allowed to stay.

"No. It's not your time," he repeated, in a firm voice that broached no argument. He told her she'd made a mistake, and that she needed to go back and help others so they wouldn't make the same mistake. The next thing she knew, she was in the MICU.

I marveled at her fluent language and her precise observations. It was so different from my own tongue-tied attempts to describe my near-death experience seven years earlier. And I thought of her mother, who'd been compelled to leave work the day of Penny's suicide attempt. Oompah was her mother's father.

After her physical recovery, Penny spent quite a bit of time in residence at the Community Mental Health Center at Harborview, learning better ways to cope with stress than self-destruction. She became a highly effective member of a teen outreach program, accompanying me on visits to area high schools where she talked about her experience and urged depressed students to seek help before trying to hurt themselves. This was in the wake of a highly publicized incident in which a boy and his girlfriend drove a car at high speed straight into a wall on Mercer Island, an affluent Seattle suburb. It appeared to be a suicide pact, and the community was concerned—with good reason—about the potential for a rash of copycat teenage suicides. Penny took on the task of helping deflect that threat, and continued her work with troubled teens for several years.

As a youthful near-death experiencer, Penny Byers was unusually articulate and composed. But she turned out to be typical in one important respect: She never attempted suicide again. Dr. Bruce Greyson, professor of psychiatry at the University of Connecticut Health Center and Director of Research of IANDS, has studied people who've had a near-death experience after trying to kill themselves. In postrecovery interviews, the vast majority state that they would never attempt to take their lives again, and would advise others against such an act. Why? Because during their experience, they became aware that what they were trying to do was fundamentally wrong. One suicide attempter eloquently expressed the understanding that she now knew that life is a gift given to all of us—a precious though sometimes painful learning opportunity for the soul, a gift given to us for growth, which is not ours to take away.

Suicide attempters who have near-death experiences also described changes in themselves that usually fall into one or more of the following categories:

They have a newfound feeling of unity with something greater than themselves—a sense of belonging in the universe. They find it easier to let go of personal problems. They discover an appreciation for the meaningfulness of life. They have a sense of specialness and a sense of purpose. They know that their spiritual essence will survive their physical death.

At Harborview, we didn't get the folks who were just playing around with suicide. We got the ones who came perilously close to succeeding. Most of the suicide attempters I counseled at Harborview really, really wanted to die. Yet I'm convinced that those who had near-death experiences in the course of a suicide attempt would never, ever try to hurt themselves again. Not because their problems went away; just the opposite. Though I, like Dr. Greyson, have observed astonishing changes in the attitudes of these suicide attempters, the problems that had made them miserable were still there after they went home from the hospital. In fact, they often found that life was even harder because death was no longer an option for them. They no longer believed they could escape their problems or their pain that way. They still had to do the lessons. They had to cope. And with help, they learned how.

I had noticed that some people who had a near-death experience did not appear to change markedly as a result; their metamorphoses tended to be more internal, affecting values and spirituality. But for others, the transformation was more dramatic. Take Mr. Lacey, an attorney in his early forties in seemingly perfect health, who collapsed on the street while walking between his downtown office and the Superior Court building. It turned out Mr. Lacey had a cardiac condition involving ventricular fibrillation, which caused his heart to beat wildly out of control. In cardiology, this affliction is known by a more descriptive term: "sudden death."

To survive ventricular fibrillation, one has to receive cardiopulmonary resuscitation (CPR) within minutes. Luckily, a passerby administered CPR to Mr. Lacey where he fell, and a Medic One ambulance raced him to Harborview, less than a mile away. He was admitted to the coronary care unit. There he began the not inconsiderable task of adjusting physiologically to the experimental antiarrhythmia drugs he was being given—and psychologically to the idea of becoming a heart patient as a relatively young man. Days later, I wasn't surprised when his wife told me she was worried because her husband seemed to be a different man. The stress of hospitalization and dealing with one's mortality affects mood and behavior in just about everyone. But I was taken aback by the rest of her complaint: Mr. Lacey had announced to her that he was quitting his lucrative law practice to serve the poor at the charity missions clustered near his office in Pioneer Square.

"That's fine for him, but what about us?" she wailed—referring, I presumed, to herself and their two teenage sons. She was terrified, with good reason it turned out, that her husband would remove them from their comfortable upper-middle-class environment featuring ski trips, private schools, and beachfront vacations, and deposit them in a neighborhood with wine-soaked alleys and a high crime rate.

When I spoke with Mr. Lacey, he confirmed his wife's fears. Yes, he planned to renounce the comforts of privilege in favor of service on the soup lines. He felt very strongly guided to do so, he said. This "guided" business sounded familiar to a near-death experiencer such as myself. But when I asked him if he had memories of anything that had happened following his collapse, he drew a blank. This man didn't even remember what year it was (1977) or what season (summer). I persisted, and asked again. In obvious frustration, he pounded his clenched fists against the steel bed rails and blurted out that he knew *something* monumental had happened to him, but he just couldn't grasp exactly what it was. What he was sure of, however, was that he had a new job to do: serving the poor.

After a few more sessions, we worked out a deal. I told him about my experience "when I died," and those of others whom I had recently met—primarily other Harborview patients. I promised to somehow get us all together to talk—for I felt strongly that we would benefit from one another's support—if he would wait one year before making any drastic changes in career or lifestyle. It was similar to the advice I gave to the newly bereaved spouses of people who died in intensive care. The first year after a loss is such an emotionally unstable period that radical decisions are often painfully regretted later. I figured the same to be true of hasty moves—especially those involving the lives of other people—made in the wake of an NDE.

Not until much later did I understand why that makes so much sense. Many near-death experiencers are infused with a completely new set of positive, less selfish values—values so important to them that they want to start acting on them immediately. Many have told me how their immersion in love gave them a "knowing" they didn't have before: that love really is the most important thing in life, and not the accoutrements we tend to value so highly. This new outlook can lead to sweeping behavioral changes that obviously have an impact on loved ones and friends. By waiting before they make any sudden moves, near-death experiencers gain the time they need to reenter and reorient themselves to what we call the "real world," so jarringly different from the one they have just experienced.

As for Mr. Lacey, he took my advice and a year later, was glad he had. He kept his law practice but donated many *pro bono* hours to people who could not afford high-priced legal representation. He joined the board of directors of a major downtown mission and lobbied the state legislature on behalf of more funding for social services for poor and homeless people. Though he was never able to remember the details of what had happened to him "when he died," he was deeply grateful for the experience. His wife and children discovered a new pride in the good deeds of the husband and father they had nearly lost.

Sometimes, the aftermath of a near-death experience is even more unpredictable, as illustrated by the case of Albert Timmer. Unlike Mr. Lacey, Timmer was not a nice man; the available evidence indicated he'd seldom been nice to anyone—at least not when he was drinking. He was an abusive alcoholic who beat his wife and children. He had few friends. He lobbed half-empty beer cans at neighborhood children who ventured too close to his property.

Timmer was such a misanthrope that his family was relieved after he keeled over in ventricular fibrillation—another potential "sudden death" victim. Unaware of his past proclivities, I waited for Timmer's wife and grown children at the ICU elevator with my trusty box of Kleenex in hand. I expected plenty of weeping, since it looked as if Timmer wasn't long for this world. But when the Timmer clan stepped off the elevator, I was met with a smiling, giggling, and joking family. No one shed a tear. The tyrant was going to his just reward, and they could hardly wait to celebrate.

Indeed, the ailing man's prognosis was poor. When he was admitted to the hospital, he looked like a turnip: white overlaid with purple. The coloration resulted from the pooling of blood while he had lain facedown for an extended time before his body was found. Brain damage can occur within six minutes after the heart stops pumping blood; death takes only a few minutes more. No one knew how long the clock had been ticking on Timmer following his collapse. I happened to be in the hallway when the medics wheeled his turnip-colored body in from the ambulance, frantically administering CPR the whole time. An exchange of glances with the receiving medical staff told me what I suspected. This guy was a goner.

But miracles do happen. Against all odds, he survived, and managed to avoid irreversible brain damage. Eventually, he went home—no doubt to a disappointed family—and returned to work. That was the last I saw of him until he showed up, many months later, as an outpatient in the hospital's cardiology clinic. Not until then did I learn of Timmer's near-death experience, and the enormous change it had wrought in his life.

To sum it up, the despot had undergone a personality change

and become a delightful gentleman. Timmer had quit drinking, retired from his job, and spent his time carving wooden toys for children. His offspring, who had once feared and shunned him, were surprised but pleased to have a sober father. I learned that he was a kind neighbor, a caring friend. Since I had never known him any other way, the full effect of the transformation was lost on me. With his sense of humor and twinkling eyes, Timmer seemed positively elflike; it was hard to believe he'd ever been so mean. So I was naturally stunned to hear that soon after he got back on his feet, his wife had divorced him.

Who knows the reasons why. Maybe it was too late for Timmer to make amends. Or perhaps his wife couldn't adjust to the new, improved version of her husband. This happens frequently. I have counseled a number of spouses of near-death experiencers who admitted they were uncomfortable being married to someone whose moral bearings had changed in midstream, so to speak. This was not the person they knew how to live with.

The Timmers caused me to think about the unexpected effects of a near-death experience—not just on the person who has it, but on everyone else. It was wonderful that someone seemed changed for what society would call "the better" by the experience. But it was like throwing a rock in a pond—the rock would hit bottom long before the ripples played themselves out on the shore. You couldn't predict where and when they would stop.

After meeting Penny Byers and Mr. Lacey in the summer of 1977, I began to see more patients who reported having had unusual experiences when they were close to death. My interest in their stories became known to other members of the hospital staff. One day, someone gave me a book titled *Life After Life* by Raymond Moody, a psychiatrist who was the first researcher to extensively "map" the experience of dying, as recalled by one hundred and fifty people who were resuscitated or otherwise recovered. This was a treasure trove for me. It also confirmed that the subject which was quickly becoming my consuming interest was a recognizable phenomenon that merited scientific attention and inquiry.

Moody catalogued the common attributes of the near-death experience, including descriptions of leaving one's body; traveling through a dark tunnel; being surrounded by light; feeling loved and at peace; meeting loved ones who had died, and seeing a montage of images from one's past. Not everyone reported experiencing all of these characteristics—I, for one, did not see my past life in review—but all of the people he interviewed experienced at least some.

Over the years, my encounters with near-death experiencers grew exponentially. Eventually, I accumulated more than a thousand interviews, and a wealth of material in need of organization. Using Moody's descriptions as a guide, plus several of my own, I devised a more detailed map of the Land of Near-Death Experience. As a clinician and researcher, I wanted to locate the landmarks and establish the coordinates with as much specificity as possible. And by showing that others had already taken this journey, I hoped to provide people with something I hadn't had— validation and confirmation: *"Yes, this happened. It happened to you, and to many other people. There's nothing to be afraid of. It's part of the human experience."*

Though individual descriptions and reactions varied widely, everyone seemed to experience the same basic phenomena. So when people said, "I never felt better"—"It was like all of the best times in my life rolled into one"—"It was like pushing away from the table after a fine meal"—"It was such relief"—"It truly was the peace that passeth all human understanding," I filed this information under SENSE OF PEACE AND FULFILLMENT and told them this was similar to many other people's descriptions.

When people said, "Everybody was yelling so loud"—"I heard someone say 'She's a goner' "—"I felt like I was trapped in a room full of hyperactive preschoolers"—"When a medic said, 'Let's hit him with a four-by-four,' I thought he meant a piece of lumber, not a piece of four-inch gauze," I filed it under ABILITY TO HEAR OTHERS and told them this was similar to many other people's descriptions.

When people said, "I heard a thousand tiny bells hanging from tree branches blowing in a soft wind"—"It was like the sound of a fan or humming light in a quiet room"—"I heard tonal qualities beyond normal earthly sounds"—"I heard a choir of angels, hundreds of harmoniously blended voices singing new and familiar hymns," I filed it under THE SOUND and told them this was similar to many other people's descriptions.

When people said, "I was floating in deep space"—"I was surrounded by gray fog"—"I just existed in the midst of unending warm darkness," I filed it under THE VOID and told them this was similar to many other people's descriptions.

When people said, "I was traveling down a tube at the speed of light"—"I sped through a long, dark cave"—"I went headfirst through a huge expanse with rounded edges"—"I returned the way I came, but backward through a tunnel," I filed it under THE TUNNEL and told them this was similar to many other people's descriptions.

When people said, "I floated above the operating room"—"I could see below to where my husband and kids were in the wreckage of the car"—"I walked through the wall and saw a nurse smoking a Lark cigarette"—"I found a pile of my missing tools on a high shelf in the garage, but I could still see myself under the car where the jack had slipped," I filed it under OUT-OF-BODY

EXPERIENCES and told them this was similar to many other people's descriptions.

When people said, "I found myself in a garden of unearthly colors"—"I was standing on aqua sand staring at two orange suns"—"Every object I beheld glowed with its own inner light"—"I saw a city of light," I filed it under HEAVENLY REALMS and told them this was similar to many other people's descriptions.

When people said, "I was pure mind, nothing else—"When I reached for my sister, my hand went right through her shoulder, so I knew whe was dead"—"I floated past the nurses' station just like a ghost"—"Wherever I wanted to be, I just thought about it and I was there," I filed it under SELF-AWARENESS and told them this was similar to many other people's descriptions.

When people said, "I saw my life like a stack of slides viewed simultaneously yet individually"—"My life went backward from the time I was injured to my birth"—"I experienced how I had affected every person's life that I had crossed paths with," I filed it under LIFE REVIEW and told them this was similar to many other people's descriptions.

When people said, "I saw the potentials for my life to come"—"I held a number of cords in my hand, each one leading to a different life possibility"—"I saw that the earth was going to shift on its axis"—"All that was to be in my life was shown to me like a sixteen-millimeter home movie," I filed it under LIFE PREVIEW and told them this was similar to many other people's descriptions.

When people said, "I saw Jesus"—"An angel carried me back"—"A being of love emerged from a light"—"Three men in plaid shirts, who were my guides, told me it wasn't my time," I filed this under HOLY ENCOUNTERS and told them this was similar to many other people's descriptions.

When people said, "I saw my wife in a ball of light and

learned after my resuscitation that she had just died"—"My foster son died of spina bifida, but even though he couldn't walk when he was alive, he came running over to me"—"I rejoiced at my reunion with my deceased parents and marveled at their youthful appearance"—"I saw my baby and that's how I knew he was a boy and that he had died when I hemorrhaged during childbirth," I filed it under MEETINGS WITH DECEASED LOVED ONES and told them this was similar to many other people's descriptions.

When people said, "God appeared before me as a Great Light"—"I saw a Light in the distance of such magnitude, all I wanted was to get to it"—"When the Light sent me back, I felt like I had been expelled from Heaven"—"The Light was brighter than millions of suns but didn't hurt my eyes," I filed it under LOVE and said, "Wow! Tell me more."

While I was still engrossed by Moody's book, our hospital chaplain dropped by to tell me about a lecture he'd attended by Elisabeth Kübler-Ross in which she mentioned meeting someone who'd had a near-death experience. (She later published her lectures on this subject in a slim volume titled *On Life After Death*.) "Isn't this what you've been interested in, Kim?" the chaplain asked. I could hardly believe my ears. Elisabeth Kübler-Ross, the Swiss doctor who is the world's foremost expert on death and dying, was my idol. Once I'd almost met her—we were waiting in line together to use the women's restroom at a hotel near the SeaTac Airport. I'd been so awed by the presence of this tiny, bright-eyed woman that I was too shy to strike up a conversation. Now her interests and mine were coming together.

That was nice. But what almost knocked the wind out of me was an overwhelming sense of déjà vu. I had the unmistakable feeling that these people whom I knew only by name "topside"—

Kübler-Ross and Moody—were already friends of mine. We'd known each other before and we were destined to meet again. I recognized them in a *flash, flash, flash* of new memories from "when I died." It was as if I had been shown a preview of my future, which I was now living. How could such a thing be? How could I remember my future?

Yet that was exactly what happened. The more I talked to near-death experiencers, the more details I remembered from my own experience. I had been told I would remember nothing except as it would become "manifest." I discovered that *manifestation*—the process of becoming evident or obvious—wasn't a one-time occurrence but a long slow revelation that unfolded in my consciousness. It was on a parallel track, so to speak, with the memories that my patients shared with me. We were fellow travelers. As I helped them give voice to their experiences, they helped illuminate mine, so long shrouded in the darkness of intentional forgetting.

CHAPTER SIX

LESSONS

▼

T
HE YEAR 1979 was a banner year for me. I began to firmly
establish my footing in the growing field of critical health
care. I bought my first house. And I fell head over heels
in love.

This was a time of intense professional satisfaction. Sometimes I loved my job at Harborview so much, I would have worked
for free. Spending time with dying people might not be everyone's
piece of cake, but it was definitely mine. From an outsider's perspective, it probably appeared that I was the giver in my relationships with patients, but in fact, I always received much more
than I gave. Not only did I feel closer to God and more in touch
with my spirituality as I sat at the bedside or in the waiting room
with scared and confused people, but I was rewarded in more
worldly ways as well.

I was promoted to a supervisory position at the hospital, and
became an instructor at the University of Washington School of
Social Work. In addition to my daily duties counseling patients
and their families, I also supervised graduate students, taught classes, and published my work in professional and trade journals. My
specialty: critical care and the role of health care professionals in
helping people deal with death and dying. The subject of near-

death experiences, however, remained largely a private pursuit, a subtext I was not yet prepared to explore publicly because of its lack of acceptance as a real phenomenon at that time.

Teaching death and dying quickly became my new passion—I couldn't get enough of it. My enthusiasm began to attract a wider audience outside the classroom. First came articles in the print media, then television interviews. In my first TV appearance, I shared double billing on a local talk show with members of the Seattle Sonics basketball team, which had just won the National Basketball Association championship. I figured I'd be lucky to get a few minutes of airtime to talk about *dying*, of all things, to an audience that only wanted to hear about basketball. But right before we went on the air, the Sonics canceled, leaving the desperate producer with an entire thirty-minute show to fill—and me as the only guest.

I was a wreck. It was one thing to be interviewed in my office by a reporter who would rearrange my words in print so I sounded halfway intelligent. It was quite another to speak at length and unedited on a live television show being broadcast to thousands of viewers. As the program began, I stood off-camera, my clammy hands squeezed into fists, praying I wouldn't make a fool of myself. At least I looked good, I thought. My platinum hair was freshly styled in a mass of shimmering curls, and I wore a knockout fire-engine-red dress. If I could be a vision of loveliness, perhaps it wouldn't matter so much what I said.

"Tonight we have someone who gets up and goes to a very different job from you and me," the host said as he introduced me. I walked onto the set repeating a silent prayer—"Thy will be done, thy will be done, thy will be done"—and was immediately greeted by an audible groan from the cameraman. I knew nothing about TV, and no one had told me that bright hues play havoc with the video image, appearing as undifferentiated blobs of color that the camera cannot "read" without making everything else on the set look dim and gray. I truly was a blinding vision, and the cameraman was having fits as a result.

Once the interview got under way, I began to relax, and occasionally even managed a witticism or two. Then, about midway through, the host dropped a bomb. "We understand, Kim," he said smoothly, "that you know a woman who has described seeing a tennis shoe on a ledge during a time she was in cardiac arrest. We'd like to ask you some questions about that when we return from our commercial break."

I felt like going into cardiac arrest myself. How did he know about Maria and the tennis shoe? I wasn't ready to divulge this story in public! In all the print interviews I'd done about death and dying, I had carefully avoided the subject of near-death experiences. My colleagues were well aware of my interest, but no one else, because I thought it might hurt my personal and professional credibility. I wanted to have a lasting impact on how people in critical-care situations are treated. I had worked long and hard to get social workers off the sidelines and on the field with other professionals on the critical-care team. Talking about "woo-woo" stuff like near-death experiences, I feared, would be distracting and maybe even detrimental to that work.

A number of critical-care nurses from Harborview had come to the television studio to watch the interview and give me support. During the break, I shaded my eyes from the bright lights and peered out into the audience to find their familiar faces. To them I pantomimed the big question: What should I say? They all gave me the thumbs-up signal to go ahead and tell the story. One nurse cupped her hands around her mouth and shouted, "Go, girl, go!" It was the encouragement I needed.

"We're back on the fascinating topic of death and dying with Harborview social worker Kim Clark, who was about to tell us about a tennis shoe on a ledge," the host continued, and the camera zeroed in on my vividly colored self. I gulped, took a deep breath, and for the first time, told Maria's story in public. The host and audience stayed with me, following every word. There were no groans of disbelief, no titters or whispers. Although this was not a call-in show, the station's phone lines lit up with interested viewer response.

That TV appearance broke the ice. I decided I could safely discuss near-death experiences outside the hospital setting without people throwing stones—figuratively speaking—or poking fun or questioning my professionalism. On the contrary, people responded with intense curiosity and a supportive attitude. Something about it rang true with them. And if nothing else, putting my name out there was bound to put me in contact with more people who'd had similar experiences, which would help my research. But I would only go so far. My own near-death experience would remain private—something I shared only with others like me. Perhaps the time would come to "go public" with it, but that time was not yet at hand.

Meanwhile, I spent weekends looking for a new home—preferably one that wasn't spooky, like the rental house where I'd been living for nearly five years. I and my newest housemate Christy Horton, a medical intern at Harborview, had decided to pool our funds and buy a house. But all we found were places we couldn't afford, or dumps in need of massive repair. We were almost ready to give up when I took yet another spin with yet another real estate agent one rainy Saturday morning. After rejecting all the houses he showed me, I was surprised when he braked his Cadillac in front of a ramshackle bungalow half-buried in a sink hole.

"Ugh," I said. "Let's go home."

"Not *that* one," he said. "This one over there." He motioned

to a charming, prairie-style, two story house across the street.
Painted slate-blue, it had a wide, covered front porch and banks
of lace-curtained windows. My first thought was that it looked
like a beautiful dollhouse. My second was that I'd seen it before.
I *knew* this house—which was impossible, because I'd never been
in this neighborhood. Memories bubbled up from somewhere.
Where? My near-death experience? The answer, I knew, was yes.
I still wasn't used to this strange feeling that I was reliving a
memory.

"I love this house!" I announced, getting out of the car to
examine it more closely. The real estate agent couldn't find the
key, so I peeked in the windows. There was a beamed ceiling, a
stone fireplace, and winding staircase. Icing on the cake, since I
already knew I was going to live there.

By nightfall, Christy and I had made a deal with the owner
to buy the house. She was a single woman, too. Her name was
Sally Darwood, and she had bought the house the previous year
and began fixing it up. Now family obligations were forcing her
to sell and move back to eastern Washington. Sally hated to part
with her dollhouse; she asked only that we let her visit her former
home from time to time. We cheerfully agreed, and on April
Fools' Day we moved in.

My first purchase for the house was a big brass bed—another
symbolically significant acquisition. Since my college days, I had
slept in beds that belonged to landlords or friends; I'd never
bought one of my own. With immense pleasure, I greeted the
delivery of my gleaming new bed, fit for a queen—or a bordello.
Too bad I would be sleeping in it alone. My love life was in pitiful
shape, mainly because of my own doing. I had been habitually
attracted to unattainable men; men who ran around like hounds;
men who needed a mother more than a lover. Lately, I'd sworn
them off altogether.

I couldn't complain; my life was full. In addition to my work, I stayed busy seeing friends, attending dance classes, whitewater rafting, and coproducing an instructional video on social workers in health care. My family, friends, colleagues, and patients all gave me warm, affirming care and support. But my heart yearned for more. I missed romantic love—great, passionate *healthy* love. I was thirty years old, and tired of waiting. So I did what I often do when I'm impatient: I took my case to a higher authority.

One night, I stood at the foot of my splendid bed, bowed my head, folded my hands, and said a fervent prayer. "Dear God, if it be Your will, please send me a great romantic love. Please bring a man into my life. Someone to love me and hold me and adore me and . . . *aarghh!* Oh, God, forgive me, forgive this selfish prayer! I'm sorry. Let me be an instrument for Your will. Thank you for all of my blessings. In Jesus' name, Amen."

I felt so foolish and selfish! How could I possibly complain about my love life when I had love in such abundance? Besides, anyone could see I didn't have time for a serious romance. Snuggling into bed, I thought of my wonderful life and my sweet, wonderful house. *Count your blessings, Kim,* I told myself. Before long, my eyes were closing, and I was reconciled—at least for now—to sleeping alone.

I slept in such utter peace in my quaint flower-papered bedroom that I kept the windows open on warm summer nights. One humid August evening, the room was too stuffy, even with the windows open, for comfortable sleep, so I had kicked off the sheets. A slight breeze picked up and I dozed off watching the lace curtains balloon out from the windowsill.

I awakened to muffled voices and strange words that sounded nonsensical. The chant was heavy and slow. Through deep grogginess I thought I discerned about a half-dozen robed, cowled figures at the foot of my bed, moving slightly from side to side as they chanted, "DAH, da. DAH, da."

The night was moonless, but a street light provided soft illumination. Unfortunately, the figures were backlit so their faces remained in shadow. I was still groggy, almost dopey. It was hard to concentrate. Why wasn't I afraid? There were a bunch of people who looked like monks in my bedroom in the middle of the night, yet I felt numbed, even restful. "DAH, da. DAH. da."

"Of course," I thought to myself, "I'm asleep. This is another weird dream." The cowled figures seemed to be both men and women, judging from the register of their voices as they chanted. Some of the monks lifted the footboard of my bed slightly and then set it down. The lifting and lowering of my bed was in sync with the rhythm of the chant, and was just disturbing enough to keep me from being rocked to sleep. I wanted to go to sleep, deep dreamless sleep. Just let me go to sleep. "DAH, da. DAH, da."

While my bed continued to be raised and lowered, monks moved from the footboard to either side of me, two at the center of the bed, two at my shoulder. With "DAH, da" as the beat, all began to chant "She wants to try, she wants to die" over and over and over. So lulling, so calming, so true. "I want to try, I want to die," I mumbled. Yes, so easy. "DAH, da. DAH, da."

As the bed rose and fell, the monks on either side of me pulled the sheet up to my chin and began to tuck it very tightly under me, binding my body in place, first at my feet, then my ankles, then my lower calves, middle calves, knees. "DAH . . ."

"WAIT!" What was that? It was my own voice, shouting. Something was wrong. I sensed . . . "NO!" I sensed energy, negative energy. Energy of despair, of evil suddenly reeked from these . . . things. "You're not monks!" I wanted to yell, but it came out as a whine as I realized that the chanting had not stopped, nor had their efforts to bind me, which had reached my hips.

In a flood of awareness I discerned that these beings were performing a ritual that was going to lead to my immediate possession, to them using me. "No possession. I want to live," I argued, but my mind began to go blank. I looked down at my body, which wrapped tightly in the sheet, looked like a mummy. "DAH, da. DAH, da."

They reached my waist, my lower rib cage. I panicked, screamed, and blindly, without thought, but with sure and swift motion reached between the beings on my left and pulled my bedside lamp onto my chest. I flipped on the switch and waved the bright light around to all sides of me, swinging it like a weapon, screaming the garbled cry of a doomed soul.

They were gone. There was no one in the room. Everything was as I had last seen it before falling asleep. The wind was still wafting the curtains. The room was empty.

It was a dream! Oh, what blessed relief! It was a dream! In one long sigh, I practically let go of all the oxygen I had. I was so happy to have emerged from that nightmarish horror. I threw my head back and let out a big laugh. "Calm down, heart," I spoke to the loudly thumping muscle. "Whew, what a nightmare!"

I lifted the lamp off my stomach from its "firing" position to return it to the bedside table. As I made the motion to turn to my side, I felt constrained. I looked down the length of my body to see that my waist, hips, thighs, calves, ankles, and feet were tightly and neatly wrapped in the sheet. My mouth opened to let out a long scream that made no sound.

*   *   *

The next day was Saturday. It seemed important to keep praying and carefully thinking. My prayers were of thanksgiving for my German Scottish roots, which I credited with giving me the stubbornness and pluckiness of spirit that enabled me to reach through those gruesome beings for the bedside lamp. In retrospect, this action made me laugh, though the laughter was more akin to whistling in the graveyard than amusement. It was kind of funny, grabbing the lamp and waving it around as though it had firing power. "Take that, you demon beings! Here's a hundred watts coming your way!"

My prayers were also for protection, which I absolutely knew had been, and continued to be, answered. The room was filled with the same movement and energy of angels as I had experienced in my parents' family room in Leawood four years earlier. Between now and then I had experienced only a vague sense on occasion that angels were around me. But in my bedroom that night I sensed numerous, not quite visible creatures standing guard. I had an odd understanding that they weren't immediately present when the soul snatchers, as I began to call them, were upon me, even after I had prayed. I somehow knew that I had needed to learn that I could confront evil on my own, that I had the faith and strength inherent within me to do so. In fact, it seemed very important that I learn that I could fight back rather than be paralyzed with fear or complacently lulled into freely allowing the possession to occur. That, I realized, was what these demonic beings had been attempting—convincing me to let go of life, to turn over to them the keys to my soul by approaching me during sleep with trance-inducing rhythms.

But why was this happening in the first place? My questions always were reduced to this one. I was sure it was related to my near-death experience, but how? When I adjusted my vision to the fog that surrounded me "when I died" so that I could discern both light and dark, did that create an opening into the entirety of the spiritual world? It had been my feeling while I was in that foggy place that I was witness to the most fundamental aspects of life as we know it—the polarities of positive and negative, love and fear, good and evil, and light and dark. Still, why were these dark confrontations happening?

My mission, I again realized. Anyone's mission, for that matter. We all cross paths with negative energy at one time or another and resist or succumb depending on our life circumstances and our use of spiritual tools, specifically prayers for protection and guidance.

Something about my near-death experience, I was convinced, had removed some of the veils obstructing my spiritual vision, which I desperately wished was really the side effect of a sleep disorder. But the body wrap of sheets that had been so carefully accomplished was as validating of the demonic visitation as the tennis shoe had been of Maria's out-of-body experience. No matter how much I tried to intellectualize or rationalize away the existence of these beings, I could only conclude that these denizens of the spiritual world really existed, that somehow they had punched through into my physical world.

The next day, I met him. The circumstances were less than auspicious for True Romance: I was up to my ears in laundry, dressed in an old faded T-shirt and shabby cutoff jeans; my hair, wadded up under a bandana; my face, without a smidgen of makeup. Our new house lacked a washer and dryer so my friend Ron Brown let me come over on weekends to use his. On this particular August weekend, Ron was entertaining friends elsewhere in the house while I plodded around his utility room in my rubber flip-flops, washing, drying, and folding. I was bent over, heaving a wet mass of clothes into the dryer when a man appeared at the back door and asked where he could find Ron.

At first, I didn't recognize him as the answer to my prayer. I knew only that this was one of the best-looking men I'd ever seen. My eyes traveled from his cowboy boots straight up a pair of long legs clad in faded jeans, past a muscular bare chest, wide shoulders, smooth jaw, sexy mouth, and deep-brown eyes—altogether a fitting package for a man whose nickname, I later learned, was Ladykiller. Part of me wanted to stay bent over in supplication to the Teutonic-looking Olympian who loomed above me—tall, lean and luscious. Too awestruck to speak, I dumbly pointed in the direction of the kitchen. With a polite "Thanks," he strolled past the piles of laundry, scarcely giving me a glance.

I heard Ron's loud voice greeting him. "Hey, George! Hi! How'd you get in?"

"Nobody answered the front door, so I came around back. Your cleaning lady let me in."

Cleaning lady? Oh no, I thought, feeling like Cinderella without a fairy godmother. I didn't have a chance!

The more I found out about George Koestner, the more hopeless it seemed. He was a German god, not a Greek one—born in Munich but raised in Columbus, Ohio. Like Ron, he was a doctor—a radiologist—as well as an accomplished pianist, indoor gardener, and expert skier. He was a challenge to some women on the dance floor because he preferred disco à la Fred Astaire instead of John Travolta. He was a veritable swoon machine: gallant, attentive, and seductive. Women forgave his sexual appetite and indiscretions because he didn't use women, but genuinely adored them. Still, his reputation as a compulsive rogue was well earned.

"He thought I was a *cleaning lady*," I whined to Christy. "Can you believe that guy? He's poison. It's a good thing I'm no longer vulnerable to men like him. I'd rather sleep with a shark than with someone who's so . . . so wolfy." I was huffing and puffing with indignation.

"Yeah, the man is a Casanova" said Christy agreeably. He was obviously wrong, wrong, wrong for me. Why was I so crazy about him?

Strange and wondrous things happen in this world; my love affair with George Koestner was one of them. We began dating in November, and by Christmas, were inseparable. On New Year's Eve, George told me he loved me, and we greeted 1980 by pledging ourselves to a monogamous relationship—more of a sacrifice for him than for me. Only time would tell whether it would last, but I was going to ride this train as far as it went.

George and I were very different. He was intense, serious, given to brooding. I was a bubbly, funny Pollyanna. He loved winter sports; I loathed them. His favorite drink was warmed Cointreau; mine was chilled Pepsi. We also had much in common. We loved to dance and were perfectly matched partners, swirling across the floor with ballroom precision without missing a beat. We shared a passion for movies, the Seattle Symphony, and any opera by Wagner. We were both such devoted fans of the flutist Jean-Pierre Rampal that we happily stood outside in cold rain to buy the best tickets to a concert. I developed a taste for Cointreau and George shared my passion for french fries—especially the hot, greasy kind from Dick's Drive-In, a popular Seattle hamburger joint. I started taking lessons in German, George's native tongue. We laughed a lot. In the first flush of love, everything we did seemed romantic and fun.

That was the winter in which Seattle, the city with a single snow plow, got buried in snow. George lived across from Woodland Park, where almost every night we tramped through knee-deep powder. It was a beautiful winter wonderland, with the enormous evergreens draped in white mantles, the sugary snow underfoot reflecting the lights of the city. "It doesn't get any better than this," George said once, surveying the magical scene. And I agreed.

George treated me tenderly, like a precious gift that had come into his life bearing light. With a flourish, he would catch me at the waist, bend me backward, and search my face with his eyes. "Who *are* you?" he'd ask. He asked me that often. He brought light into my life, too. I wasn't afraid of sleeping in the dark when I was with him. Even on nights when I slept at home alone, thoughts of George kept the bogeyman far from my consciousness.

Had I known how long we'd have, would I have done things differently? Probably not. Retrospect may be the mother of regret, but I have few regrets where George and I are concerned. I gave him my best shot; I think he did the same for me. There's not much more you can ask for. Except time.

Our last week together began on a strangely unsettled note. It was a Sunday evening in March; I lay in George's arms on the couch in his darkened living room as we listened to an hour-long broadcast of a prerecorded radio show on death and dying. I had a special interest in the program, in which a University of Washington professor of bioethics and I discussed grief, terminal illness, and life after death. The discussion worked well, and I wanted George to hear (and praise) every word. But as the hour progressed, he grew suspiciously quiet. Then he began to snore. I was so proud of this program, and there he was, sawing logs! I knew that all new doctors are chronically sleep-deprived. But he could have tried! I was seething with anger.

When the program ended, George's eyes flew open as if he'd heard a shot. I let him have it. "How could you fall asleep?" I demanded. "I told you how much it meant to me. I know you're tired. I know you work hard, but so do I, and I managed to stay awake."

If George heard my tirade, he didn't respond. He was staring through me, as if hypnotized by something far beyond either of us. He seemed completely unaware of my voice or my presence. My anger gave way to concern. "George? George, what's the matter?" I asked. "Are you OK? You look like a ghost."

George apologized and gave me a long hug, but he was different after that night. Though his personality was intense, I'd always been able to bring out the humor in him and make him laugh. Now he was solemn and distracted. Yet he was hyperaware of everything around him, stopping in his tracks to note the way raindrops clung to a fern, or the shape of a cloud or an unswept cobweb in a corner. His sleep habits changed, too. From that Sunday night on, George clung to me as if we were braided, in a way that felt more like desperation than romance. It made it very hard for me to sleep. If I moved away from him during the night, he would stir and pull me back, as if he could not bear to be parted from my touch, my smell, my breath.

The following Tuesday, we visited a planetarium exhibit at the Pacific Science Center. George was particularly taken with the constellation Cassiopeia, and when we left the building, he searched for it and found it in the night sky. "I'm giving you this constellation," he said meaningfully. "From now on, these are our stars. And as long as they are in the sky, I want them to remind you of me."

That was a romantic thought, but the serious tone of his voice worried me. "Why?" I asked. "Are you going somewhere?"

"Yes," he answered. "I'm going to Dick's for our french-fry fix. Any objections?"

On the way home, as we polished off the french fries, the radio played "This Is It" by Kenny Loggins. This was "our" song because of its theme of love and committment, and when we heard it, we usually bounced up and down like kids and sang the words loudly to each other. This time, though, he didn't join in the duet. He kept both hands on the steering wheel, staring fixedly at the road, not a trace of a smile on his lips. I belted out the song by myself with a kind of grim determination. These mood swings confused me. On the one hand, George seemed more in love than ever—bequeathing me a constellation, no less—and on the other, I sensed he was pulling away. I sang the same words to the song, but what I really meant was: "Please don't leave me."

The next night, we went skiing in the nearby Cascade Mountains with a mutual friend. (Skiing was another activity I was learning to enjoy with George.) Near Snoqualmie Pass, we hit a blinding snowstorm that brought traffic to a halt. After half an hour, the snow began to let up and I recognized where we were on the mountain. Years earlier, a friend's fiancé had died when his car had skidded on ice and went off the cliff on the opposite side of the road. Tired of sitting in George's van, we got out to look at the accident site while we waited for the highway patrol to open the pass again. We crossed the road and stood staring over the edge into the snowy abyss. Finally, our friend broke the silence. "I want advance warning before I die," he said. "A chance to say good-bye. A long illness would suit me. I want to know what's coming."

"Not me. I want to go just like this. Send me right off a cliff."

George snapped his fingers and added, "I want to die *this fast*."

It seemed to be my turn next. "I already know how I'm going to die," I said. "I found out in my near-death experience." This was the first time I had admitted this glimpse of the future to anyone. I explained that I had had a vision of my death occurring sometime before my thirty-fifth birthday in the crash of a white plane. That was all there was to it; I didn't know where or when or under what circumstances, but I was absolutely convinced of the clarity of my vision.

George and our friend looked stunned. George knew I had had a near-death experience, but we had never discussed the details and certainly not this one. I tried to lighten the mood. "Hey, I'm sorry to upset you guys. Maybe what I saw isn't necessarily going to happen. It may just be potential, not written in stone. I want to live a long, long time—with you, I might add," I said, putting my arms around George. "But to be honest, if it happens, I won't be afraid. I'm not afraid of death."

George and I didn't speak of it again until we got back to his apartment. Then we proceeded to stay up the entire night talking about my near-death experience. George's curiosity was exhausting. Over and over again he asked me what it felt like to die. Over and over I told him what I remembered. He was relentless, pulling information from me that I had not fully processed myself. Not until we left for Harborview the next morning did he run out of questions.

That evening, I attended my Thursday night German class, and George spent time with his best friend, Andy. When we got together later at his apartment, he seemed frustrated. He said he wanted to tell Andy something but Andy wouldn't listen to him. When I asked him what it was, George brushed it off as nothing. But he muttered about it until it was time for bed.

George planned to leave Friday afternoon on a weekend

cross-country ski trip to the Olympic peninsula. I was attending the funeral of one of my patients on Saturday, so I wouldn't be going with him. We had lunch together at McDonald's a few blocks from the hospital. We talked for two hours, blessedly free from interruption by either of our beepers. Once again, George was in communication overdrive. He began by confessing the experiences in his life that he was not proud of. He said, "I want you to know everything about me. And I want to know anything about you that you haven't told me."

There was only one thing—the demon that had plagued me before I met George. I told him everything. To my surprise, he took it in stride, nodding as if he understood why a demonic presence would haunt me. At one point in the conversation, I told George that we seemed to be mentally and emotionally re-gurgitating. "No," said George. "We're bringing the darkness into the light." Afterward, we walked back to the hospital with our arms around each other, bracing ourselves against a strong south-westerly wind. Out of the blue George looked down at me and said, "I don't think I'm going to go away this weekend."

"What do you mean?" I asked.

"I don't know. I just have a bad feeling."

I reminded George that forty people in his ski group were depending on him to drive his van, loaded with their skis, to the Olympic Mountains. "That's true," he said. "I don't know how else they're going to get those skis over there." We walked the rest of the way to my office in silence. George leaned down and kissed me good-bye, long and hard.

"Hey, maybe you should go away more often," I said, laughing, and kissed him back. He didn't say good-bye—he just smiled and winked and walked down the hall. A few moments later, I was startled by his reappearance in the doorway to my office, still wearing his red down ski jacket, his brown hair whipped around and his cheeks ruddy from the blustery weather outside. He was staring at me as if he wanted to memorize every detail.

"I'll be seeing you," he said. Then he was gone.

A wild storm blew into the Puget Sound area that afternoon, beginning with thunder and lightning and ending with hail, rain, and snow. Traffic slowed to a crawl on the highways as I inched my way home to West Seattle, where I was meeting a friend for dinner at a neighborhood restaurant. Suddenly, a scene took shape in my mind. It was vividly clear, but with an ethereal quality, like a hologram. I saw a man's body buried under the snow— a man wearing a red ski jacket. It was George.

I cried out in horror. The scene faded away. What was *that*? I tried to shake it off, concentrate on other things. But the wall had been breached, and thoughts, frightening thoughts about George, poured through the gap. I couldn't ignore them. George was in terrible danger: I knew it. I needed to call him, or call someone who could tell him not to drive to the mountains. But there was no way to get off the freeway that fed the bumper-to-bumper traffic on the two-lane temporary bridge into West Seattle. I wanted to abandon the car and flee in search of a phone. Instead, I told myself, "Get a grip, Kim. This is nuts."

Every minute that passed was filled with anxiety and dread. When I reached the restaurant, I ran for the pay phone and dialed George's number. The phone rang and rang in his empty apartment. Tears blurred my vision. I grabbed the phone book and began calling everyone I knew who was planning to join him on the ski trip. No one answered.

My friend Kathy Fair met me at a table in the restaurant and saw immediately that I was agitated about something. As soon as she sat down, I blurted out, "I think George is going to die tonight in an avalanche!"

Kathy was dumbfounded. I tried to explain. "This is crazy, but I had a vision of George dead in the snow. I know it was him. He's gone skiing, and I think he's going to die." I apologized for obsessively focusing on George, but it became harder and harder to think of anything else, like food. What to order? How could I eat? It was hopeless. Finally, I told Kathy I had to go home. "This is crazy. I think I'm going crazy. I'm so sorry. I have to get out of here."

Christy was on call, so I went home to an empty house. I paced every inch of the floor; I couldn't keep still. Walking back and forth, I wrung my hands and talked to myself out loud: "George is dead in the snow. George is dead in the snow." I tried to calm myself with every coping mechanism that had worked for me before. I picked up the phone to talk to friends, but no one was home. I worked on crossword puzzles and took a long brisk walk. I wished I had some of Dick's french fries. Yes, that was it—it was Dick's fries I needed. No, it wasn't worth the trip. Again I paced. Again I called and listened to phones ringing. My anxiety mounted. I had a repeat of my earlier vision of George dead in the snow, and I howled in pain. I cried until there were no tears left.

In a trance, I climbed the stairs to bed. I slipped into my well-worn flannel nightgown and went through the motions of washing my face, combing my hair, brushing my teeth. I was beyond pain now. I knew in my heart of hearts I was never going to see George again.

Slowly, numbly I walked to my bed, got down on my knees, and bent my head in a posture of prayer I had not used since childhood. With every fiber of my being I begged God to please bring George

CHAPTER SEVEN

THROUGH THE VEIL

▼

G EORGE DIDN'T DIE in an avalanche. He was killed when his van crashed on an icy road west of Port Angeles on the Olympic peninsula. He took a curve too fast—he'd gotten a speeding ticket earlier that night—and the van skidded on bald tires over an embankment. The load of skis in the back broke loose and at least one of them hit George in the back of the head, breaking his neck. The autopsy showed he was already dead when he went through the windshield. It happened "just like that," as fast as a snap of the fingers, the way George had wanted it to. The three passengers who were with him survived.

The accident occurred around midnight—precisely the time I called my sister on the phone and was overcome with a feeling of peace. It took the emergency personnel a while to find George's body. He had been thrown into a snowbank and was buried in the snow. His body was found as I had seen it in my vision six hours before the van left the road. I had seen it, but I couldn't prevent it. No one could.

After George's memorial service at the University of Washington Medical Center, I visited his apartment one last time. In the bedroom, two pillows lay side by side, still molded with the impressions of our heads. Never again would that bed feel the weight of our bodies on it. I looked at the piano that George would never play again. In the stack of mail, I saw a card that I had sent him on the Friday he had died. I slipped it into my purse, vowing never to open it. I even saved the newspapers so I could find out what else had happened on March 15, 1980; I wanted to know who had died and who had been born. I needed to remind myself that there is a rhythm to life: the coming into this existence and the leaving for another one, itself a kind of birth. One of the newspaper articles warned cross-country skiers and snowshoers to beware of freakish weather on the ides of March—"they could be as fatal to you as they were to Julius Caesar."

My father met me in Kansas City and together we flew to Columbus, Ohio, to attend George's funeral service. Paying our respects at the funeral home the evening before the service, we were greeted by George's tall, courtly grandfather. He invited us to view the body. Now came my moment of truth. I had seen countless corpses in my five years at Harborview, many belonging to patients I cared about deeply. But I'd never seen the corpse of a loved one, and I'd been dreading it all the way to Columbus. It would mean the end of the last vestige of denial that George was really dead. But I also needed to come to grips with the fact that this man whom I loved was now lying in a box in the next room, ready for burial.

As we approached the sapphire-blue coffin, I thought how much George would have liked that color. With every step that we took toward the coffin, I wanted to stop. But although this was my last chance at denial, it was also my last chance to say good-bye. My mind and my heart wailed out, "George, George how did it come to this? How can you be in that blue box?" Then we were next to the coffin. I looked inside. Relief flooded through me. It wasn't George. It was George's body, but it wasn't George. The real person, the real soul, the real loved one was not inside.

It was so clearly a shell that I began to laugh. A heavy weight lifted from me. As I studied George's features for the last time, I took note of how dashing he looked in his dark blue pin-striped suit. The last time he wore it was on New Year's Eve when he had first told me that he loved me. I then announced, "George is not here," and walked away.

Dad and I returned from the funeral home to our hotel by the airport. We said good night and went into our adjoining rooms. I put on my nightgown, got ready for bed, and turned on a light in the bathroom. Stepping back into the darkened bedroom, I saw something move to my left on the dresser. It was the demon, sitting with his knees drawn up to his chin.

The air in the room thickened and liquefied. I could hardly breathe, not from fear, but from shock. For a split second, the demon remained in human form, then leaped from the dresser toward me, transforming in midair into a reptilian beast. I pushed against it, but it grabbed my shoulders and threw me onto the bed. Grabbing it with both hands, I pushed back with all my strength. Somehow, I knew the beast meant to enter me through my chest, above my heart, in an act of possession.

Flashes of insight came to me as we struggled. I knew that the demon had been waiting for grief to weaken me. I also knew that I was wrestling with a fundamentally negative energy that could assume any form it chose—a man, my sister, a reptile, a clanking chain. With a giant heave, born of adrenaline, I pushed against its body long enough to lock my left ankle around part of the bed. Using the bed for leverage, I pulled myself into a seated position and we fell on the floor. I had to stay off my back and keep its jaws away from my chest. My strength was fading as the demon's will fought mine. We wound up on the bed again and he shoved me onto my back. I knew the struggle was over.

Yet in this moment of utter helplessness, I was flooded with divine awareness. In the midst of this awareness, I remembered the part of me that was a child of God who would always belong to God. I gave my ebbing will entirely over to my Creator at that moment. Out loud I cried, "Oh, Lord, my heart is ready!" I did not call out for God's intervention with the demon, because I was ready to go to God. I was ready to die. I had no choice. I determined no creature of evil would take me.

A new feeling of empowerment suddenly infused me. I was immediately filled with a spiritual strength I had not known before. With my left arm, I pushed the beast's head away from me and stood up on the bed. Grabbing the beast's throat with my left hand, I spoke with a loud, commanding voice in the language of the Holy Spirit. The demon writhed in fury at me. Encircling my left leg, it began scratching me frantically trying to wrench its way from my grasp. I would not let go. My whole countenance had changed. I was filled with a holy, invincible righteousness.

Into the upper right corner of the darkened room came a wedge-shaped band of angels. Without counting them, I knew that there were thirteen. They were enormous, perhaps ten feet tall, radiating light. These were not cute, cherubic Christmas-card angels, but furious-looking warriors with long, burnished hair and billowing white robes. They wore fierce expressions I would never, ever want directed at me. I vowed that if I were ever tempted to step outside of the circle of God's love, I would re-member their countenances.

Still speaking the language of the Holy Spirit, I commanded the angels with the full authority of God. I reached behind me with my right hand, which now held something that I gripped like a handle. I never turned to see what it was. I held the writhing beast by its throat at arm's length with such power that it loosened its grip on me. The angels descended around us as I brought whatever it was in my right hand down on the demon.

The room was suddenly empty.

There was nothing in my hands, right or left. I was breathing heavily, still standing on the bed where the battle had occurred. Was the demon destroyed? I don't know, but I knew that it was removed forever as a threat to my soul. It was over.

I remembered my dad. Was he OK? Had he heard the battle? I quietly opened the door that separated our rooms. In the darkness, I heard his peaceful, rhythmic breathing. I smiled at the knowledge of his safety and my own. I closed the door, walked into my bathroom, and confidently turned out the light. In the darkness that echoed the sleep that was to come, I returned to my bed and fell into a deep slumber. There would be no reason ever to fear the darkness again.

The next day dawned dark and cold. Steel-gray clouds hung over Columbus, spilling sheets of rain outside the cathedral where George's funeral took place. I had been reluctant to disclose the events of the preceding night to my Dad, my spiritual confidant. But, as with my near-death experience, I kept close counsel. I was so needful of Dad's emotional support that I did not want to risk alienating him on any level.

My father and I sat in a back pew and watched the pallbearers carry George's casket down the aisle, followed by his family. During the service, the priest talked about the eternal realm, and how "time for George in heaven is far different from how we perceive time on earth. Ten years for us will be naught but a twinkle in George's perception of time." I knew this to be true from my near-death experience. Out of our physical bodies, time does not exist as we know it; instead of past and future, there is a profound sense of "now."

As I thought about the priest's words, I heard a familiar voice—George's voice—say, "Hi, Kim!" My mouth dropped open and I spun my head around. "George?" I said. But of course I saw nothing. My dad squeezed my hand reassuringly. In a moment, I heard George again, as if he were simultaneously behind me and inside my head. He told me what I already knew—that only his body lay in the blue casket. The real news was that his spirit was in the next pew.

I was so happy I wanted to jump up and yell, "George is here! George is here!" His presence felt so real that I was convinced George was not only attending his funeral but providing color commentary. He teased me about our seats in the back of the church, which he called "the po' folks' section." When praise was heaped upon him in the eulogy, George remarked dryly: "Obviously, this guy never knew me." In life, George was rarely funny, but in death, he became a regular "jokemeister." I sensed his loving spirit moving around the cathedral, visiting other mourners with a gladness of heart that was palpable. It was incongruous that the only happy soul among all these sad and weeping people was the man whose death we mourned.

After the funeral mass, my father and I joined the procession of cars to the cemetery south of town. The downpour had let up, and as we walked to George's gravesite on the crest of a ridge, I ceased to feel his presence. My feelings were all mixed up. Part of me was still in shock as I realized George's body was about to disappear forever into the cold ground; part of me was joyous that I had sensed his closeness at the funeral, and part of me doubted my sanity. Staring at the flower-bedecked casket, I listened to the priest's last words with a growing sense of unreality.

When it was over, and Dad and I had walked down the hill to our rental car, I was suddenly seized with an urge to turn around and go back. "I'll be right back," I said as I started up the steep incline again. "I'm coming with you," said Dad with a note of fatherly concern in his voice. We stopped halfway up the hill and took one last look at George's gravesite, surrounded by funeral wreaths. Everyone had left. A sharp gust of wind swept the hillside, exploding the wreaths everywhere and blowing the bower off the coffin. All earthly adornments stripped away.

"It's all dust in the wind," George told me. This time, I didn't need to look around for him. I could feel his essence within me; our souls were closer than they'd been even during our most intimate moments together. Then his spirit departed.

"Good-bye, George," I said. Profoundly grateful for the chance to have this final leavetaking, I took my father's hand and we walked away.

Unfortunately for the living, accepting the death of a loved one is not a one-stop process. The full weight of my loss bore down heavily on me after I returned to Seattle. The thought of being at Harborview and not seeing George was unbearable. My appointment book was filled with dates we had planned to spend together. All I had of him now were memories and a few pictures and plants which I was given from his estate. I took to my bed, immobilized by depression, rousing myself only to talk to my partner in despair, George Wertz.

George Wertz had lost his wife, Mary, the same week George Koestner was killed. Mary, a coronary care nurse from another Seattle hospital, had been one of my patients. She had collapsed as a result of a brain aneurysm and never regained consciousness during her long, inexorable decline in intensive care. We had all fallen in love with Mary—not only because she was about our age and as a nurse was "one of us"—but because of the wonderful stories her family and friends told about her. They brought alive a vibrant personality we could only guess at, trapped in a body that had failed her.

For a period of time, George Wertz and I clung to each other like dazed survivors in a life raft. To prod ourselves to get on with the business of living, we made a pact: We would phone each other every hour or so to report what we had managed to accomplish during that time, no matter how trivial—opening the mail, doing the laundry, moving a body part. In the beginning, our conversations went like this:

"Kim, this is George. What did you do?"

"Well, I almost took a shower."

"Good, good."

"What did you accomplish, George?"

"I scraped food off a plate into the garbage disposal."

"Did you turn on the disposal?"

"Yeah."

"Great. You're doing better than me."

Before returning to work, I was afraid I wouldn't be able to stand being around other grieving people, that I would overidentify with their pain and become ineffectual as a counselor. My job at Harborview—my patients and their families—had been my refuge in times of personal stress, but now I worried that I would not be able to endure working where death was a constant presence. I didn't have much time to ponder the potential difficulties, though. As soon as I walked in the door my first day back at Harborview, I was paged to the surgical intensive care unit.

"What's the problem?" I asked, automatically pulling myself together.

"We admitted a fellow who was in a car accident this morn-

104
▼

ing," the nurse told me. "His fiancée just arrived and the patient has just died. We're swamped, all the docs are in O.R., and our social worker is out sick. Will you go to the waiting room and inform her of his death while we clean him up? She can come in in about fifteen minutes."

The nurse, an acquaintance who obviously did not know of my personal situation, dashed off without waiting for an answer. I took a deep breath and read the patient's chart. In the waiting room, I introduced myself to a woman who resembled me in age and appearance. With an assurance born of long experience, I sat down with her and told her how the accident had occurred, how badly her fiancé had been injured, and how hard the medical team had worked to save him. By my facial expression and voice tone, I was letting her know there would not be a happy ending. The more I talked, the closer I moved to her. By the time I told her that her boyfriend's massive head injuries had been fatal but caused little suffering, I had my arms around her. As she sobbed on my shoulder, I quietly said, "I know how you feel."

It was then that I knew George's death would not impair my work but facilitate it. As I had with near-death experiencers, I was able to connect with the newly bereaved on a deeper, more spiritual level as a result of what I had gone through. Perhaps it didn't make me a better social worker, but it did make me a more caring one. And by helping others with their grief, I was—little by little—easing my own.

Exactly a month after George's death, I attended a baby shower for one of the ICU nurses. During the course of the evening, I became increasingly distracted by the same blissful elation I had felt at George's funeral. Was George close by again? No, I thought—probably just an unconscious wish for his presence set off by the anniversary date. I tried to brush it off, but the feeling persisted.

Driving home, I began to sense George's voice. It was odd because I wasn't hearing him as I had before—I was *feeling* his voice. It felt like he was trying to tell me something, but I couldn't understand what it was. I slept fitfully during the night, awakening often and asking aloud, "What? What?" Still there was no answer.

Dressing for work the next morning, I thought of little except the incessant "knocking" on my consciousness, as George's attempts to communicate with me became more persistent. *Knock, knock, knock, knock,* like a woodpecker that wouldn't stop. In exasperation, I finally said aloud, "Listen, I'm a real cement head. I'm sorry. I know you want something. I don't know what it is. I don't get it. Give me a sign, something I can understand. Give me a memo."

Upon reaching my office, I immediately saw a pink piece of paper on my desk with the word MEMO printed boldly across the top. Beneath it was a message reminding me to "call Andy" and an unfamiliar phone number. Phone messages at Harborview were usually written by the secretary on pale-green slips of paper; this note was not in her handwriting nor from her notepad. I dialed the number anyway and George's best friend, Andy, answered the phone. We had not spoken since before the funeral.

"Andy, hi, what a surprise. This is Kim."

"Hi, Kim. How are you doing?" We made polite conversation for a while, then there was an uncomfortable pause. Finally, I asked Andy why he'd called. He replied that he was returning my message to call him.

"What message?" I asked, puzzled.

"I'm looking at it on our kitchen chalkboard right now. It

says, 'Call Kim,' " and then gave the number for my department. That was my work number, all right.

"Andy, I didn't call you until just now. When did you call?"

"A while ago. I talked to the secretary."

I put him on hold while I checked with the secretary for messages. She told me that I had a few in my box and proceeded to read them off. The last message was from Andy.

"What color is the paper that it's written on?" I asked her.

"What color? It's light green."

Our standardized message forms did not have the word "MEMO" printed on them, much less the screaming bold headline that was staring up at me from the piece of paper bearing the Andy message.

"What time was the message received?"

She read a time that corresponded with Andy's estimate of when he called. As I stared at the paper while we talked, I noticed that the hot pink memo was timeless. And it was not written in the secretary's handwriting.

I got off the secretary's line and was just getting back to Andy when I began to feel the bliss that signaled George's presence. Before I knew what was happening, his spirit seemed to melt into mine. We were not only sharing body space but every aspect of being. My thoughts were now our thoughts. My feelings were our feelings. We were completely connected.

I remembered how disturbed George had been the night before the accident when he told me he'd tried to tell Andy something, but Andy wouldn't listen. Now I understood that George had unfinished business with Andy, and that he could not continue on his spiritual journey until it was taken care of. It was up to me to be the conduit between these two.

"Look, Andy," I said. "I don't know how to explain this to

you, but George is here and he has something to tell you."

This clearly made Andy uncomfortable; I could tell he was anxious to get off the phone.

"Andy, I know this is weird. I'm sorry to distress you, but I think George wants to get your attention." Suddenly, I saw a scene, as if a giant photo slide were projected on a screen in my mind. Now I knew how to get Andy to listen to me instead of hanging up.

"Andy, I see you seated to my left. We're in a car. Your hands are resting on the lower part of the steering wheel. I'm looking at a brick wall in front of the car. To the left is a roadway where a few cars pass by. There's a streetlight shining on a small footbridge going over the road."

I heard a sharp intake of breath. "That's where George was sitting, in the seat next to me in my car, and that's what we were looking at as we talked. It was the last time I saw George," said Andy.

Now it was George's turn to talk, and talk he did, using my voice. It felt as if I were sitting in the backseat of a car that George was driving—strange, but not frightening. He was entirely in control and the conversation belonged to him. I didn't formulate or communicate any thought of my own, even though I talked for some time. Though I was aware of the words I spoke, they lacked such relevancy to me that when it was over, I couldn't recall exactly what had been said. The gist of it was that George loved Andy, but they had both been too macho to discuss their feelings for each other. There was deep satisfaction on George's part when he was finally able to communicate this to Andy. He had completed his unfinished business with his best friend.

But George wasn't ready to leave just yet. For the next ten days, I continued to be acutely aware of his presence, which I began calling The Bliss. It opened me up to a spiritual realm that seemed to exist between heaven and earth, where George's spirit had apparently taken up temporary residence. The Bliss removed all communication barriers so we could hide nothing from each other. The good, the bad—all was revealed. I came to know George better in death than I had in life, and I saw—truly saw—our relationship for the precious gift that it was, as well as what it was not.

Because George died when our relationship was at its romantic peak, I had idealized it as perfect, unblemished by the little irritations and disappointments that emerge over time. Such perfection, of course, cannot be sustained. Ruefully, I learned from George that despite our love for each other, he and I would not have made a successful lifelong fit. He would not have been faithful to me, which would have hurt me deeply, and we would not have had children, which would have been even harder to bear. Over the long haul, we would have caused each other much pain. I didn't question this knowledge that George relayed to me; I didn't ask how he knew these things. For as much as I loved and missed him, I also knew he was telling the truth.

None of this deterred me from my wish to dwell with George forever—on a spiritual level. The Bliss lifted me from the depths of depression to a constant state of heightened spiritual awareness and euphoria, affecting me in surprising ways. For one thing, I developed a heightened sensitivity to others that bordered on the telepathic. This came in handy at work, such as the time one of our cardiac patients began behaving so irrationally that she was referred for psychiatric services. I visited with her and by "reading" her mind, immediately knew that her problem was chemical, not mental. I asked a medical resident to check out the combination and dosages of medications she was being given for her heart condition. Sure enough, the drugs had caused a toxic re-action that triggered psychosis. The medications were adjusted and her psychosis disappeared.

I had always been empathetic and quick to connect with someone else's wavelength—one reason I was good at my job. Now this talent progressed beyond mere empathy. I could tell by touch which patients would live and which would die. I was aware of people's thoughts and emotions as they passed me in the hall or on a sidewalk. I knew personal facts about total strangers; I sensed whether they were alcoholic or grieving or gay. I didn't ever feel judgmental. If anything, I felt more compassionate. I *understood.*

My awareness expanded to what felt like a cosmic under-standing of the universe, much as it had during my near-death experience. I saw the patterns and crucial connections in science and history. It seemed as if I could instantly count all the stars in the sky, all the flowers in a garden, the grains of sand on the shore. We are always being bombarded with information in our daily lives, but we filter much of it out. I filtered nothing; I took it all in, every scrap, no matter how trivial or irrelevant. The result was I began to feel a little crazy and overwhelmed, like a switchboard operator with too many incoming calls. And as I became more and more absorbed in spiritual life, I forgot to eat, forgot to sleep. In comparison to the strange and wonderful events occurring in my awareness, those basic activities seemed trivial, a waste of time. I was a whirling dervish, on the verge of spinning out of control.

One morning at five-thirty, I was awakened by the piercingly beautiful sound of a bird singing outside my window. Ordinarily, I'm not a morning person—or a bird person, for that matter—but I was instantly wide awake. I got out of bed and walked down-stairs to the kitchen in search of something, but with no idea what it was. Then I spotted it. Sitting on the counter, silhouetted in the faint dawn light cast through the kitchen window, was a bag of Dick's french fries. Not only that, they were still warm.

How did they find their way here? I'd cleaned up the kitchen before going to bed, and Christy was on overnight call at the hospital. Feeling like Alice in Wonderland when she saw a piece of cake with a sign saying EAT ME, I bit into one of the warm, salty fries. Unlike Alice, I didn't shrink with every bite, but began to come down from my dizzying altitude of spiritual consciousness. I devoured the entire bag. I could feel myself calming down, regaining my practicality. This Bliss business was exhilarating, but I had been reckless. To adequately perform my daily responsibilities, I had to pay attention to my physical and mental well-being, too. The fries were a reminder ("Earth to Kim! Earth to Kim!") to come down from my spiritual high and restore some balance to my life.

Thank you, George.

A few nights later, I was sitting at the table in my candlelit dining room writing a letter to George's favorite aunt, when the phone rang. It was my friend Laurie Simpson, crying as if her heart would break. A dear friend of hers had just been killed in a car accident. I tried to console her, telling her about people who'd been badly hurt in terrible car wrecks, who remembered no pain or trauma as they lingered near death, but only feelings of peacefulness, love, and an utter lack of fear.

I read Laurie a letter I had recently received from a woman in Olympia, Washington, named Margaret, who'd been widowed in World War II. She recalled receiving news of her bereavement, in 1944, in a roundabout way, after the car in which she was riding collided with a truck. As she lay unconscious, she found herself rising above the wreckage and entering a tunnel. To her surprise, her husband, who had been fighting with the army in France, now joined her. Together, they moved toward a great, loving light. Her husband entered the light, but Margaret was pulled backward through the tunnel and into her own body again. That was when she knew her husband had died. Three days later, a uniformed messenger brought a telegram to her hospital bed informing her of his death in the Battle of the Bulge.

The point of this story was that death is only a physical separation, not a spiritual one. Laurie's friend, like George, was likely close at hand, wanting to comfort her and let her know that she would be all right. I wanted to tell her how George's presence had comforted me, but she was too griefstricken to hear more. We said good-bye, and I felt a tremendous pain pass through me, like wind through a curtain. It was the pain of Laurie's loss and confusion, but I felt it like my own.

As I turned once more to the letter I was writing, the pain gradually gave way to anger and doubt. Why was I penning these ridiculous words of optimism, assuring George's aunt that while her beloved nephew had departed this world in the flesh, his soul endured? How did I know George's spirit was with me? Had I actually *seen* him? Did he hold me, touch me, laugh at my jokes as he had in life? What did I mean, telling Laurie Simpson that her friend was close by? Her friend was dead and gone, just as George was. And what did I know about eternal life? Maybe we were destined for worm food, nothing more. From nothing we were born and to nothing we returned; everything that happened in between was the luck of the draw. Some were just luckier than others.

This explosion of doubt sent me into an emotional tailspin. Who was I to presume to give lessons in healing? I was wounded myself, and my recovery was by no means certain. Was all our

travail part of God's plan? If so, I didn't see the point. My voice
rose in the chorus of mankind's oldest lament: If there is a God,
why would He let us suffer so? My anger grew. Out loud I shouted,
"I don't believe any of this stuff anymore! I don't believe that we
are eternal souls! Those who live, live; those who die, die. I believe in nothing!"

God must have taken me seriously. Instantly, I was plunged
into a formless dark void. There was an absence of everything,
including time and space and God. I floundered there for what
seemed like forever, in the emptiness that signifies the absence
of love and faith and purpose. The most hellish part was that I
lost God's companionship. I missed it. I desperately wanted it
back. I promised that I would never again doubt God's presence,
God's plan, God's perfection.

Sometime later, I found myself sprawled across Christy's bed
upstairs. I had no idea how or when I'd gotten there. Downstairs,
the candles had burned out and my letter lay unsealed on the
dining room table. I was so happy to be out of the void that I
said thank you to every object I saw. Reading the letter over
again, my words no longer sounded false or hopelessly naive. They
were the truth that I knew. I believed George's spirit survived, as
surely as I had survived my own encounter with physical death.
I believed the grave merely marked a stopover in the journey of
human existence, not the end of it.

My vulnerability to moments of deep, wrenching doubt surprised me. When we are hurt and in pain, it's easy to lose ourselves in a slough of despair and negativity. Asking for help from
God lifted me out of my self-created hell. Once again, I witnessed
the greatest power, the power of love, manifested through God
in us all. The crisis of faith was over.

CHAPTER EIGHT

MIZPAH

▼

G EORGE'S PRESENCE became an integral part of my life—
almost as if he'd never left. I didn't behold him as the
classical ghost depicted in literature and movies. He
didn't appear in the form of his physical self, or even as a shimmering mist. I knew when he was around mainly because of The
Bliss. He was with me most of the time. I sensed him when I
awakened and as I fell asleep. He was with me in the car and at
Harborview as I made my rounds with patients.

I wondered if it would be this way forever. The answer was
no, as I soon discovered. But first, George and I had some work
to do—a final collaboration on behalf of our mutual friend,
Kenny Brown. Kenny was the brother of Ron, in whose laundry
room I had originally met George. Though still a young man,
Kenny was old before his time. His lifelong battle with diabetes
had left him blind and frail—he eventually lost the use of his
legs, too—but it had not crippled his spirit. Even after his sight
failed, he kept his job in a Dallas bar, pouring beer and cleaning
off tables by feel. Kenny was charming, funny, deeply kind and
loving to all he met. He was the kind of guy who was unperturbed
when a guest wildly swung a pool cue and broke a valuable ce-
ramic sculpture. "I'm so relieved that somebody finally did that.

Now I don't have to worry about it breaking anymore," Kenny said.

One afternoon, I dropped by Ron's house to see Kenny, who was temporarily staying with his brother. Our visit had barely gotten underway when I felt The Bliss, and I knew George was with us. I wanted to tell Kenny, but announcing the presence of a dead person isn't easy to work into a conversation without stopping it altogether. So I began by describing George's funeral, and the incidents that convinced me that George had been present among the mourners.

Kenny took this information in and remarked, "I do believe I feel George is next to us right now. He probably has his feet up—if he has feet." We both laughed at the thought of George hanging out with us, draping his long legs over the furniture. I got up and stood at the picture window that overlooked the Seattle-Vashon Island ferry run on Puget Sound. As if on cue, a white ferry was making its way toward the terminal at the bottom of the bluff below Ron's house.

"C'mere, Kenny," I said, pulling him to my side. "I feel a metaphor coming on." Together we stood at the window, and I described the view he was unable to see. "There's a ferry boat down there on the water. It reminds me of life. The people riding in the boat are looking at the mountains, the sky, the water, the other people on the boat. They call what they see 'reality.' Some people peer over the rail and look down at the water. Most of them can't see past the surface—the reflection of the sky and the clouds; the waves, the froth stirred up by the boat. But just below the boat is an entirely different world, full of drama—birth, death, struggle, war—as well as peaceful coexistence, and it contains at least as many different species as there are above the water. They've got mountains, valleys, seascapes of endless variety. That's the reality for the creatures in that universe. Sometimes, one of those creatures might look up and see the distorted images of other beings beyond their reach—the people leaning over the ferry rail. That's all they know of us.

"All that separates these two worlds is a thin veil of molecules. It's the only barrier between these two parallel realities— one in air, the other in water. Some creatures in the air world have special equipment which temporarily allows them to enter the liquid environment and observe other life forms; likewise, certain water creatures can temporarily emerge and see for themselves the nature of life beyond that molecular barrier. But for the most part, the two realities seldom intersect, and the inhabitants of each have little firsthand knowledge of how the others exist.

"It's the same with spiritual life," I continued. "There is just a thin layer separating what we call reality in this world from another reality which we call the spiritual. Spiritual existence is just as real as the world beneath the surface of the water. And like the people on the ferry who look down and see nothing in particular, many folks do the same regarding the spiritual world. They might presume nothing is there, only random reflections from their own reality; the familiar ripple of waves upon the surface. They miss the teeming atmosphere that's right under their noses."

I told Kenny that some people have special gifts which allow them to perceive the spiritual world for a while. And some spiritual beings have the power to visit our reality, which I call "topside." We recognize our topside reality through our five senses—sight, hearing, touch, smell, taste. The spiritual reality is infinitely more complex; it engages senses that we don't even have names for, in ways we don't have language to describe. To glimpse it is a gift and a blessing.

As I waxed more rhapsodic, the setting sun hit the water with such intensity that a blinding reflection of sunlight burst into the living room where we stood. Kenny grabbed my arm as if he was losing his balance. "I can see it!" he exclaimed, a look of radiance on his sightless face. "I can see the light! I can see the boat! Oh, God, I can see it all!" But Kenny was talking to God, not to me. I knew that in a flash he understood everything I had said and that his consciousness was ascending along an upward spiral of awareness.

To my surprise, a spiritual empowerment came over me, filling me with sacred authority. Just as when George's spirit had entered my body and melded with every cell, so was I now filled with the Holy Spirit. I turned to Kenny, who wordlessly knelt in front of me with his head bowed. Both hands reached for my right hand, which he placed on his head. Then I blessed him, using words that no one had ever taught me, that I simply knew. It wasn't me, Kim, doing the blessing; it was God coming through me. As my hand rested on Kenny's head, I understood that whatever his lot in life, however long it might be or whatever hardships might lie ahead, God loved him dearly. I knew that Kenny's gallant bearing of his suffering would inspire others and touch many lives. This blessing was God's message to Kenny that he was cherished beyond measure. I felt blessed, too, because I was witness to this sacred, intimate moment.

That seemed like enough spiritual activity for one day. But an even more startling experience awaited me. Driving home from Ron's house in the Green Weenie, I was thinking about Kenny and how grateful I was to have spent time with him that afternoon. Suddenly, the steering wheel and dashboard began to dissolve before my eyes. In their place, billowing from under and around me as in my near-death experience, was the Light— brighter than the sun, filling every space.

I remained completely conscious. I was still driving the car.

I remembered that I was in perfect health, that I was not in physical danger, and therefore, this was not another near-death experience. At the same time, the Light filled me with ecstasy. The Light was love—immeasurable and unconditional. It swept me up and took me in. The effect on me was rapturous, euphoric, even orgasmic, but not sexual. It felt like a holy union, a marriage with God.

The knowledge that I had acquired "when I died" flooded my consciousness again. In the twinkling of an eye, I remembered everything about everything, from the personal to the universal. And I remembered George. I saw and heard him perfectly—not with my eyes and ears, but with my heart. George told me to carry on the message of God: that He loves us and is with us always. That life is for learning and is a wonderful gift; that there is no end to our loving relationships nor death for our eternal souls.

He told me that it was time for him to leave and go to God. His mission on earth was over. I had been part of his mission and he had been part of mine. Our relationship gave us both experiences that helped us on our journey through life and enabled us to help others. George had helped me push my limits and realize that real love is boundless and infinitely giving. Our love had brought me pain, but the pain also forced new spiritual growth and understanding.

The Light faded from the car, and so did George's presence. Behind the ragged peaks of the Olympic Mountains, the sun had long set. The trusty Green Weenie was idling at a curb on the street where I last remembered driving, and the steering wheel was back in its rightful place. Later, I learned that I'd been in the car for more than three hours. Driving the rest of the way home, I took stock of what had happened during the past few months. I had received love and given it. I had slogged through the depths of sorrow and ascended the peaks of joy. I had been tested. I had felt The Bliss and witnessed miracles. I had helped a blind man see to the "other side." In my hands a steering wheel had dissolved into holy light and a french fry became a sacrament of love. The world was indeed a strange and wondrous place, as Maria and George and so many others had taught me.

It was April 23, 1980—the beginning of another new chapter in my life. I was going to miss George, but now I knew both of us would be all right. His spirit had gone, and this time it was for good.

After my encounter in the car with the presence of the Light of God, I felt reborn. I spoke of it romantically, longingly, counting the hours, days, weeks, and months marking the anniversary of when I had last been in God's presence. It proved equally as powerful as my near-death experience—only this time, of course, I wasn't in physical danger, or even close. Back in 1970, I'd had no point of reference and no language for what had happened to me. Now I knew enough about near-death experiences to recognize the car episode as the same sort of transformational spiritual event, with similar after-effects. For instance:

I beheld everything with new eyes. It seemed God had reached into my heart, into my entire being and had taken me to a place where I was cleansed and rinsed of all negative energies in the shower of God's love. After being in the presence of the Light, I understood what it meant to know—really know—the preciousness of life and the importance of living life fully through appreciation. Everything I encountered seemed extraordinary. Were flowers ever so beautiful? Did fir trees always smell so good? Had the sun always slid behind the mountains with such spectacular beauty? Where I might have been too busy or distracted to notice these details before, now I gratefully lingered over them. I also became more loving and demonstrative, to the point that some of my friends gagged on my frequent and lavish bestowal of hugs, kisses, and "I-love-yous."

I had an increased sense of invulnerability and the absolute belief in the special importance of my life. I had already lost my fear of death when I nearly died in 1970, so that didn't change. What was new was this feeling of specialness. This reaction is well documented by researchers such as Russell Noyes, Jr., whose study of near-death experiencers shows that many express a similarly powerful belief in their indestructibility and personal destiny. "In psychological terms, these changes might be summarized as heightened sense of omnipotence, experienced affectively as a feeling of invulnerability and cognitively as a belief in continued existence, and as increased self-esteem, experienced cognitively as a belief in the special importance of one's life," writes Noyes in *The Near-Death Experience: Problems, Prospects, Perspectives.*

As a result, I felt at ease with myself, as if I had completed a supercondensed, instant form of psychotherapy. I was braver, boldly seeking out adventures that in the past would have intimidated me. I was more willing to "go with the flow" and accept people—even people very different from myself—as they were. Material possessions became far less important; instead, I craved new knowledge, new experiences. In June of 1980, three months after George's death, I took a leave of absence from my job, cut my long platinum hair and dyed it brown, bought a backpack, and took off for Europe. For several months, I traveled, mostly alone, through Greece, Germany, France, Yugoslavia, Italy, and Holland—a trek that continued the quest I had begun when I came west from Leawood, Kansas, ten years earlier.

Strange coincidences wove themselves with increasing frequency into the fabric of my everyday life. It could be as silly as wishing for a cookie and having it magically appear on my desk, or as serious as having a long-lost friend in Central America contact me shortly after I prayed for help in finding him. Ask and you shall receive. I received so often that I became downright cocky about my ability to summon up, say, a parking space whenever I needed one. I had to yank hard to keep my ego in check—to remind myself that I personally couldn't take credit for arranging such fortuitous happenings but was merely the instrument whereby a higher power pulled the strings. There were other spiritual occurrences as well. Sometimes I saw angels, or sensed the lingering presence of a deceased patient. I jokingly called all such odd events "woo-woos," for lack of a better term. When Seattle near-death experiencers started using the same playful term, a friend respelled it *wu-wu*—an acronym for Wild Unexpected Wonderful Upheaval.

My sense of mission was reinforced. There was no longer any doubt in my mind—if it had ever existed—that I was meant to serve not only the dying and those afraid of death, but people who were trying to make sense of unsettling spiritual occurrences: near-death experiences, woo-woos, and the like. I wasn't sure how or when this mission would be accomplished, but I was more certain than ever before that it would be my life's work.

There was a big catch attached to my mission: I had to overcome my reluctance to appear foolish, weird, or just plain crazy. To minister effectively, I needed to acknowledge and respect spiritual and mystical events that strained the credulity of people who could not see beyond their topside reality. Most of us—myself included—have a natural fear of looking ridiculous. I could not allow myself to be distracted by embarrassment if I said or did things that I knew in my heart were necessary, but appeared bizarre or inappropriate to someone else.

One of the cases that helped give me confidence in such

situations was that of Donna Higgins, a former Harborview social worker who was diagnosed with brain cancer shortly before George's accident. Donna went downhill fast. I did not know her well, but when I heard that Donna's cancer was terminal, I went to visit her at the hospital where she was a patient.

There's a common misconception that because medical personnel have what might be called a working relationship with death, they lose their own fear of dying. In fact, they are as afraid as anyone else—often, more so. Despite her professional expertise, Donna was terrified of death. Her close friends had rallied around her, taking turns in a round-the-clock vigil in her hospital room so she would not be alone. Because I was merely an acquaintance of hers, I felt out of place. But I knew there was nothing to fear about death, and it was more important to tell Donna that than to worry about intruding on an intensely personal situation.

Donna was conscious but unable to speak well. Her eyes would open for a few moments, then close again as if she were very tired. When they were open, she seemed fully alert and aware of who was in the room and what they were doing. She was aware of my presence but did not acknowledge it with a smile or a greeting. I approached her bedside and told her I was sorry about her illness and I prayed that she was comfortable. I explained that I had come because I'd heard that she was afraid that death would be the end of everything, that there was no form of consciousness after our last breath. Her brow knitted—not because she was confused, but because she seemed to have trouble hearing me.

I looked around the room at Donna's friends, who were staring at me as if wondering who this weirdo was. They must have been shocked at my next move: I climbed into bed with Donna so I could get my mouth right up next to her ear. I told her what

I knew about the "other side," and about the testimony of others who'd been there. It wasn't a fearsome place but a glorious one; everyone said so. Mainly, I told her about the wonderful Light of God that she would see when she died. All she had to do was follow her heart, and her heart would guide her to the Light. I tried to ignore the murmured comments of disapproval coming from behind me. Some of Donna's friends apparently felt I should not be talking to Donna about her death. But I was confident I was doing the right thing. She died peacefully not long after that, with her loved ones at her side.

A few months later, I was on a plane from Paris to Athens when I sensed Donna's voice call my name from a seat in the row in front of me. Turning my head slightly to the left, I caught a glimpse of her, or rather her spirit. She appeared in transparent, fluid form, as if she was made of glass or water. (Many years later, when watching the movie *Predator*, I was fascinated by the special effects which enabled the Predator character to appear as transparent as Donna had.)

The plane was coming in for a landing, and for a brief moment, I shifted my glance out the window at the rapidly approaching ground. *Wham!* It felt as if someone had grabbed my chin and turned my face back around. Donna wanted my attention. Though no one else seemed to notice the spirit presence on the plane, I was riveted by Donna. She had something to tell me. I wasn't sure what it was, but I sensed she simply wanted me to know she had made it to the other side, and that I had been right. There was consciousness after death, and she was the embodiment of it. Her message delivered, she simply faded away. The next thing I was aware of was a heavy jolt as the wheels of the plane hit the runaway.

Perhaps it's strange to recognize a spiritual connection within the context of a Hollywood movie, but several movies have affected me this way. The most important was Steven Spielberg's *Close Encounters of the Third Kind*, which I first saw in September 1980 after returning from Europe. It was a *very* long evening at the movies because I sat through it once, twice, three times—crying, laughing, awestruck. Why? Because even though the theme was supposed to be about encounters with extraterrestrial beings, to me it felt like a movie about my near-death experience.

I related so strongly to the characters who had witnessed the unidentified flying objects. Substitute the elements of a near-death experience—the out-of-body experience, the encounter with the Light, the sense of rebirth—and you had the same sort of life-changing impact that Richard Dreyfuss and the other actors so artfully depict. The movie is exactly on target in showing the skepticism of those who have not shared the experience; its dividing effects on the family, and the emotional bonding with others who did have the same experience—who truly understood. Oddly, I was more taken with *Close Encounters* than *Resurrection*, a movie which came out the same year and actually is about a woman's spiritual rebirth when she nearly dies. The heroine is an immensely strong individual who overcomes long odds to survive, and then becomes a healer. I had a hard time identifying with her—perhaps because I didn't feel I was that strong a person.

My near-death experience so affected my perceptions that I began to see one of my favorite movies from childhood—*The Wizard of Oz*—as an allegory. The tornado is the archetypal tunnel; the black-and-white beginning and ending of the movie represents the three-dimensional "flatland" of our earthly world; the fantastical and sometimes nonsensical adventures of Dorothy in Oz, filmed in splendid color, resemble the ineffability of the near-death experience. Finally, the dismissal of her journey by her loved ones ("There, there, Dorothy. It was all a dream.") is achingly similar to the reaction of skeptics who prefer to label the experience as a meaningless dream, a symptom of brain dysfunction, a hallucination. Poppycock. This condescension does Dorothy no favors, or any of us trying to make sense of our lives following a transformational, mystical experience.

I needed movies to distract me in the fall of 1980, because I was mourning another death—that of my beloved grandmother, Tyra Lueking. The indomitable, selfless Tyra had been my mentor and inspiration all my life. She made sure that even as a child I understood the value of serving and tending to the forgotten people in our society—the poor, the aged, the disabled. She shook up my comfortable middle-class complacency with our forays into the heart of Kansas City's urban darkness. She had me read to blind people and sing to people in nursing homes who had no visitors. One of the few songs I knew from beginning to end was "How Much Is That Doggie in the Window?" and that was what I sang.

I was my grandmother's first grandchild and her favorite. She always told me we had a pact: Whoever died first would greet the other in heaven. "We have eternity together," she promised. As a token of our special love, we exchanged half medallions that matched each other to create a whole disk, like sweethearts wore in the 1950s. Hers was inscribed with MIZ, mine with PAH. Mizpah was the name for the biblical benediction "May the Lord keep watch over you and me when we are away from one another." The Lord did keep an eye on Tyra, who managed to survive a radical mastectomy for breast cancer in her eighties. When the surgeon told her she had a type of tumor that was not likely to recur for at least ten years, she smiled broadly and replied, "Oh, doctor, that's wonderful! I'll be dead by then!"

As usual, Gram was correct. Her heart just stopped, right in the middle of her favorite soap opera, *As the World Turns*. While helping the family sort her belongings, I looked long and hard for her medallion, but never found it.

Mizpah, Gram.

CHAPTER NINE

THIS LITTLE LIGHT
OF MINE

▼

T
HE 1980S MIGHT have been the decade of greed, but for
me, it was the decade of angels. I have always been fond
of angels, or guardian spirits, but they weren't exactly regular visitors of mine. That changed after my second experience
in the Light, which seemed to open a door in my consciousness
to these spiritual beings. I began to see them everywhere; not
only "my" angels, but other people's angels, as well as angels
attached to no one in particular—all-purpose angels you might
call them.

One of my first sightings came out of the blue, so to speak—
actually out of a fierce storm on the Washington coast. I had
flown to La Push, a fishing village, with a friend in his single-
engine Cessna. We parked the plane at an abandoned airstrip
and put-putted into town on the little motorcycle he'd brought
with us. When the storm blew in, he decided to go back and
check on the plane. As I watched him leave, hunkered down on
the scooter in the teeth of a gale, it occurred to me that he could
use some angelic protection. At almost the same moment, an
angel appeared, sitting right behind him. I couldn't believe my
eyes. My friend and the angel were both crouched in the same
position, knees drawn up, heads into the wind. The rain beat off

my friend's back, but it went right through the angel's, who looked like something out of an angel book: classic white robe, white hair, pale skin, and a lump around the shoulder blades which might have been folded wings, but I wasn't sure. My friend seemed unaware of his riding partner, and he later returned safely.

In the meantime, sitting alone at the motel, I wondered how this vision came about. I had not prayed about it, or meditated. I had not performed a ritual. And I most assuredly had not been drinking—yet I had seen an angel. As I watched the waves crash on the beach, a very strange thing happened: I saw more angels. There was one out by a rock. Another was near a man who was bent over, walking into the wind on the beach. I discovered there was a trick to it. If I let my eyes slide out of focus a bit, like when you're trying to make out the image within a Magic Eye mosaic, I could see what was hidden beneath the surface of my vision. I could see angels all over the place.

I saw angels hovering over Interstate-5 at rush hour, as if to protect those drivers who were not thinking even remotely angelic thoughts as they honked horns, cussed, and tailgated the drivers in front of them. I saw them at the oddest times, such as at the Health/Science Fair I attended at the University of Washington Medical Center. Just above the heads of all the people milling around exhibits in an atrium there was a huge congregation of angels. They looked for all the world like angels at a cocktail party—not flying, but standing in small conversational groups. I blinked my eyes several times. I tried to think of something else. I focused on the unlit pipe of a man a few feet away from me. But when I glanced back at the ceiling, they were still there: relaxed, chatting, seemingly oblivious to me.

Like the other angels I had seen, they were bigger and taller than most humans; they wore robes and often had wings. (Yes, wings, which were folded decorously at their sides.) They had an ethereal, transparent quality, like the spirit of Donna Higgins I'd seen on the plane, yet they seemed fully a part of what we recognize as reality. They were *right there*—they'd been there all along, but in a parallel dimension we're not used to seeing.

In all my angel observances, which lasted for several years, I never tried to get their attention and I certainly never prayed to them. After all, they weren't *my* angels—they were God's. God knows when we struggling humans need angels and provides them accordingly. They protect us, guide us, and encourage us, but they serve at God's beck and call, not ours.

Like my other extracurricular spiritual interests—near-death experiences, demons, and ghosts—the appearance of angels was not exactly an approved subject for chitchat with acquaintances. I made an exception, however, for Elisabeth Kübler-Ross. In 1985, Elisabeth came to Seattle to appear on a television show that featured a number of terminally ill children and their siblings. Afterward, she was a guest at my house for a dinner prepared by one of her admirers, a man who later died of AIDS. Despite her celebrity status, which I held in awe, she was gracious and charming, as unpretentious as the casual clothing—corduroy slacks, cotton flannel shirts, Birkenstock shoes—that she preferred.

After dinner, she and my other guests and I talked late into the night. Someone brought up angels, and I mentioned that I sometimes saw them. This aroused Elisabeth's attention. "Do you see angels around me?" she asked.

"Yes," I answered, guardedly. This was still weird for me to discuss, even in the presence of the individual who bore primary responsibility for lifting the taboos that characterized American thought about death and dying.

"What do you see?" she asked.

I looked at her and adjusted my field of vision so I could see the angels more clearly. "Well, they're big sons of guns, and I think they're male. Maybe two of them."

She stared evenly at me without saying anything. After a momentary pause, the conversation drifted to other topics. Only later did I learn that Elisabeth was already fully aware of her "spooks"—her disarmingly candid term for her angelic helpers, or spirit guides. She also knew they were male, and even had names for them.

As you might expect, angels appeared frequently in the hospital setting. One of the most dramatic incidents involved a physician named Saul, who was a patient in the coronary care unit. Saul knew as much about heart disease as any of the doctors working on him; the staff respected his knowledge and all were very fond of him. We all knew, as did Saul, that he was terribly sick.

I was paged to the CCU the day Saul went into cardiac arrest. Standing off to the side so I wouldn't be in the way, I watched the frenetic resuscitation activity around Saul's bed. At one point, the medical team paused in their efforts to see if Saul could maintain any cardiac activity on his own. The pair of hands that had been performing CPR froze above Saul's pale, naked chest, fingers interlocked and palms together. We all stared at the flat line that immediately formed on the electrocardiogram machine. "Continue CPR!" shouted the doctor in charge.

But before anyone could make another move, Saul shocked us all by opening his eyes wide and sitting straight up, like a puppet bending from the waist—a surprisingly energetic motion for a moribund sixty-year-old man. He stared out the doorway behind me with such an astonished expression that I turned to see what he was looking at. Coming toward us was a group of angels, so many I couldn't get a head count. Their faces wore expressions of pure beatitude and love, directed straight at Saul.

132

No one else in the room appeared to see them. With a tiny smile on his face, his eyes still open in wonder, Saul fell back on the bed. I knew he was dead, just as I knew he had truly seen, in the words of the old spiritual, "a band of angels coming after me/ coming for to carry me home."

During the early eighties, I first became aware of increasing interest in spirituality and the near-death experience within the health care profession. I was surprised by the big turnout for my first formal presentation on the topic to health care professionals—the Western Washington conference of the American Association for Critical Care Nurses. The room was full of nurses who listened intently to the stories I had been compiling from my work at Harborview. It was nurses who spent the most time with patients, who had far more intimate knowledge of their psychological condition than the doctors. (This is well documented, according to Melvin Morse, a Seattle-area pediatrician and author of best-selling books on the near-death experiences of children. Studies that track activity in intensive care units show that the sicker patients become, the less time physicians spend at their bedside.) The nurses' intense curiosity about the near-death experience and its aftereffects reflected questions and concerns that had developed from their own observations; they were hungry for more knowledge about the subject.

They weren't the only ones. Along about this time, Melvin Morse was still in his pediatric residency when he got interested in near-death experiences. During his rural medicine rotation in Idaho, he had treated a little girl who had almost drowned. The clarity with which she recounted events that had taken place while she was profoundly comatose, as well as vivid details of her visit to a place she called heaven, whetted Morse's scientific curiosity. With a grant from the National Cancer Institute, he wanted to study near-death experiences in children. Knowing of my interest in this field of inquiry, he asked me to help conduct the research. Our subjects were young patients at Seattle's Childrens' Hospital and Medical Center who had been in life-threatening situations. To date, it remains the only study of its kind.

When Dr. Jim Swan, a psychologist, visited Seattle to deliver a lecture on "Mystical Experiences," I eagerly attended, and was lucky to get a seat in the standing-room-only audience. That was where I first heard the term "supra conscious," which Swan used to describe an intense mystical event which is experienced in the form of very bright light, which in turn is recognized as complete, unconditional love. Most people, said Swan, attribute the Light to a being of incredible holiness. He was describing my experience exactly!

More confirmation came within the pages of *Life at Death* by University of Connecticut psychologist Kenneth Ring, the first researcher to take a hard scientific look at the near-death phenomenon. He estimated that in the United States, 35–40 percent of people who survive cardiac or respiratory arrest have recollections that fit the description of a near-death experience. Ring analyzed data from his interviews with more than a hundred near-death survivors whose accounts were strikingly similar, regardless of whether their brush with death resulted from accident, illness, or a suicide attempt.

A few months later, I delivered a lecture to another conference of nurses from eastern Washington and Idaho—and my lecture career was off and running. The presentation included prepared remarks and a slide show, but what everyone most wanted to hear were the stories. I talked about people who'd had out-of-body experiences, who'd gone through the tunnel, encountered the Light, seen deceased loved ones, watched their life in review like an old-time newsreel. I told them about Penny Byers, about Mr. Lacey the lawyer, about Dusty and John.

Dusty and John were a devoted couple who were going through a sad time: Dusty was a hospice patient, suffering from the final stages of cancer. Perhaps due to stress from dealing with Dusty's illness, John had a massive heart attack. While he was being cared for in the emergency room, his heart stopped. He felt himself leaving his body and viewing the commotion in the emergency room from somewhere near the ceiling. He was then distracted by a ball of light coming his way from another dimension—a place not only outside the hospital, but outside the world as John knew it. The ball of light grew bigger and closer until it got right in front of him. It opened up and there stood Dusty.

She appeared to be silently beckoning to him. John said *beckon* was not a usual word in his vocabulary, but there was no other way to describe her body language. Her arm was bent upward, palm facing John, and she slowly moved it from right to left and then from left to right. He couldn't tell if she was saying hello, good-bye or "Hey, look at me." He remembered that he was delighted to see her. She had a very loving smile on her face and she hadn't looked that healthy in months. When he reached out for her, she was quickly enveloped in the ball of light and disappeared.

The next thing John knew, he was back in his body, looking up at the worried faces of several doctors and nurses. "Dusty's dead! Dusty's dead!" he shouted to them. "No, no," someone reassured him. "We've talked to her nurse. She's resting now— she's still alive." They sedated John to calm him down. When he awakened that evening, his cardiologist was at his side to give him the sad news: Dusty was, indeed, dead.

John recovered from his heart attack and went home to pick

up the pieces of his life. But his near-death experience nagged at him. It became very important to John to prove the truth of his vision: that he had really seen his beloved wife in the afterlife. To do this, he needed to document precisely when Dusty died and when he had gone into cardiac arrest. Methodically, he gathered the information. An emergency-room nurse had noted the time of his cardiac arrest; John took it down. The hospice nurse had called the county medical examiner's office, as required by law, when Dusty died. John got a copy of her notes, and the records from the medical examiner. He laminated copies of these documents and carefully put them in a three-ring binder. Somehow, it was a great comfort to preserve the truth, in black and white for all to see: Dusty had died and his heart had stopped only a few minutes apart.

Perhaps someone with an engineer's mentality, like John, needed palpable evidence. But I was hearing so many accounts of mystical experiences that almost nothing sounded strange or weird or unbelievable anymore. Occasionally, I ran across someone who I suspected prevaricated or exaggerated, but this was the rare exception. People were far more prone to withhold, even dissemble the details of their experience than to disclose them fully and thereby risk censure or disbelief. For many of them, groups such as the International Association for Near Death Studies (IANDS) offered their first chance to speak freely and openly of these life-changing events.

In the spring of 1982, I helped reorganize the Seattle chapter of IANDS, which is now the oldest and largest group of its kind in the world. Four of us met around a living room coffee table, and the first order of business was to share with one another the experience which had led us to that meeting. Never the shy, retiring kind, I went first. Then, one by one, the others told their stories.

Betty Preston had nearly died during heart surgery. An em-
bolism, or air bubble, had blocked the passage of blood to her
brain, damaging her eyesight, limiting function on the right side
of her body, and destroying a decade's worth of memories. What
she never forgot, however, was her near-death experience, which
she had written and titled "The Intradimensional Me." It was the
first I'd heard of someone having company in the tunnel; Betty
not only had human companions but animal ones. She read aloud
from her account:

> Around and around . . . as if I were traveling through a
> tunnel . . . easily . . . gently. It may have been swift but
> could have been like a blink of the eyes. I was not afraid.
> A long journey perhaps. It was a comfortable one. I was
> aware of other people and creatures . . . I was also aware
> of my past life. It was like it was being recorded—maybe
> like being put on a computer (for recording purposes).
> There was the warmest, most wonderful love . . . love all
> around me. There were two beings who came to see me.
> They were as delighted to greet me as I to see them. They
> were two of my closest friends, both deceased. They ex-
> tended the most beautiful understanding. There may not
> have been voices. There was complete communication.
> We were bathed timelessly in the happiness of our eternal
> friendship. They are my guardian angels.

The group reflected on this. Was it possible that after we're
finally dead, we would have the opportunity to welcome those
we'd loved on earth? ("Hi, honey, long time no see. Thought
you'd never get here.") This was actually a secret desire of mine—
to be an eternal social worker, a meeter and greeter in the afterlife. My musing was interrupted by Betty's soft voice:

I felt light-good-happy-joy-at ease. Forever-eternal love. Time meant nothing . . . just being. Love . . . pure love. The light was yellow. It was in, around, and through everything. It is what halos are made of. It is God made visible in, around, and through everything. One who has not experienced it cannot know its feeling. One who has experienced it can never forget it, yearns for its perfection, and longs for the embodiment of it.

Every cell in my body tingled as I remembered my own experience in the Light, and the sadness of leaving it. How much better Betty had described that loss than I had! There had been nothing else—not the loss of George, nor my grandmother, nor any of my patients, nor anyone I had loved—that caused me more grief than being separated from the visibility of God's love in the form of that perfect, brilliant Light. I knew how Betty felt.

And I also knew the consternation she felt when she heard her son Ron calling her, his voice booming so loudly it sounded as if it were coming over a public address system: "Mom, come back. I love you, Mother, I love you more than anyone else in the world." Her son's love and faith brought her back, despite her desire to stay in that wonderful place. She, too, chose life.

Joan Berryman spoke next. An attractive woman in her mid-thirties, the mother of two young girls, she bore scars all the way up to her lightly freckled face from third-degree scald burns. It was in the course of surviving that life-threatening burn that she had the near-death experience which she described to us. She, too, had encountered the Light ("ten thousand times brighter than the sun") and remembered sensing music. "I didn't hear the music—I felt it, like waves."

She explained that she had passed through a wall, knowing that it was composed mostly of space. The most solid objects contained only tiny particles of matter floating in space. She examined a hand. Was it her own? Joan didn't recall. But she saw the skin and muscles and bones simultaneously—saw all of it, though even an X-ray machine could not. "Surfaces did not block my ability to 'see.' I was aware of the blood moving through the veins and also aware of the cells that made up the blood as well as the molecules that made up the cells. The limitation of my senses was lifted. I could perceive reality as we know it exists, but cannot normally see it."

Joan had hit upon something else that I knew was true, but found difficult to explain. When I entered the gray, foggy place during my near-death experience, I knew I was in a place that existed in the real world, though I couldn't recognize it at the time. I think that's because the fog consisted of subatomic particles—a soup of matter that forms the basis for the physical world—which cannot be seen without an electron microscope. The fog was light and dark, energy radiated and energy absorbed, the yin and yang of quantum physics.

I have no scientific bent and never took a physics course, but one day, I picked up a nature magazine that explained quantum mechanics in very elementary, simplified terms. By the time I finished, I was in tears. Why would this particular article affect me so deeply and emotionally? I think it was because it took me back to the foggy place, where I was filled with the awe of creation and where I achieved an understanding of the universe that has eluded me ever since. The damnable thing about a near-death experience is that most, if not all of it is ultimately ineffable. There are simply no words in any language to adequately express what happens to our consciousness when we die, or almost die.

Caroline Graves's near-death experience had happened many, many years ago. Though she was now approaching seventy years old, her hair was still dark brown and her face nearly unlined. She calmly told how she had entered the hospital for a simple appendectomy and was given a new kind of anesthesia called an epidural, or spinal block. But the anesthesiologist was inexperienced, and sensation in her lower body was not fully deadened. When the doctor's scalpel sliced into her abdomen and exposed the viscera, she began screaming, "I can feel that! I can feel it!" Someone quickly clamped a mask over her face and gave her ether. She plummeted into a darkness as black as velvet, total darkness, nothingness.

It seemed to her that she began to float, as light as a feather, free of all her cares. "I was utterly free and joyous," she told us. She floated along very close to the ground, over what appeared to be a well-worn path, wearing a long white robe that completely covered her feet. The air around her was as clear as crystal, purer and sweeter than any air she'd ever breathed before. The sky was a vivid blue with a few lacy white clouds. Everything was quiet. She had never known such happiness and peace.

Ahead of her the path almost disappeared as it sharply dropped down among boulders into a deep canyon. Caroline hovered there, looking about. She heard voices, many voices, calling to her from across the chasm where a group of people was gathered, making strange gestures in her direction. Her sister, who had died a number of years earlier, stood in front of the group. She was holding Caroline's stillborn baby daughter, whom Caroline had never seen. To her surprise and delight, she recognized relatives she had never met in her life, including her grandparents on both sides of her family. How did she know these people were her kinfolk? She just knew, the same as she knew the baby that had been taken from her at birth.

Caroline longed to get over the chasm to hug and kiss them and feel their arms around her, but they did not seem glad to see her. She couldn't understand their seeming rejection, especially when she was filled with joy at the prospect of being with them. What was the matter? Why were they motioning her to go away? Her sister's voice carried over the chasm, faintly, a long thread of sound that Caroline struggled to unravel. Then it got louder— her sister always had a very loud voice—and the message got through. "G . . . o . . . baaack," her sister was yelling, the words all strung out. "Go back. It's too soon. Too soon. It isn't time." The others echoed her words like a chorus: "Go . . . baaack . . . too . . . soooon," they said, gesturing frantically. "It isn't time yet."

Sadness came over her. She didn't want to go back, but she turned slowly away. Then she found herself in a great dark tunnel being propelled at terrific speed toward a blinding golden light. She was just about to crash into the light when she slammed back into her body. Her eyelids fluttered open. Someone was holding her hand. She could hear someone crying. A voice said, "She's going to make it," and she looked up into the eyes of her husband. She had been unconscious for three days.

The four of us discussed what it was like to survive a near-death experience in a culture that looks askance at spirituality and transformational experiences that cannot be rationally explained. A culture that labeled us as nutcases—or worse. I told them about a woman I had once seen in the psychiatric lockup unit at Harborview, and the dismissive comment made by a medical attendant: "Oh, she thinks she's been out of her body." Yet none of the hundreds of near-death experiencers I've interviewed have been diagnosed as psychotic.

We counted our blessings that we had not fully shared our near-death experiences with many people—none, besides ourselves, that we didn't already know well. Those memories were too precious, too sacred to expose at the risk of rejection or ridicule. I told the group that in my numerous lectures throughout the state of Washington, I had not once revealed to an audience that I myself had had a near-death experience. I could not fathom being that intimate with a roomful of strangers. Besides, I still feared such a revelation would undermine my credibility as a serious health care professional, and as a result, undermine my work. I wasn't surprised when the three other women agreed. We had all long ago realized it was prudent to keep quiet on this subject, to protect ourselves and our loved ones from other people's ignorance, prejudice, or condescension.

Joan reminded us that we were explorers of sorts, recounting spiritual journeys that shed new light on the nature of reality as we know it. Some of these stories echoed the great mystical experiences in religious history. We decided there there would be one place, at least, where people could speak freely of these matters in a supportive and accepting environment—and that place would be the meetings of Seattle IANDS. We needed to break out of our self-imposed isolation, to share our experiences with others and encourage them to share, too.

The next month, twenty-five people showed up at the meeting, drawn there by word-of-mouth. Living rooms became too small to hold us all, and we soon moved to the basement of a branch of the city library. When we outgrew that, we settled into an even larger facility, in central Seattle. Although we do almost no advertising, our monthly meetings usually attract from a hundred to a hundred and fifty people. Interestingly, the vast majority—about seventy percent—have never had a near-death experience, although they may have experienced the death of a loved one. They come for many reasons: as a means of dealing with their grief; a desire to know more about mystical experiences; just plain curiosity; or perhaps other reasons that they don't fully understand themselves.

Guests may be surprised that these meetings are upbeat. But

we come together not just to explore the meaning of the near-death experience, but to share a common knowing that we walk, breathe, and laugh in spiritual dimensions as well as the other three. This is our common ground and a cause for celebration. Some people arrive at the meetings with differing religious definitions, ready to be drawn, but most of those are left at the door. Inside, the near-death experience creates a larger context in which to savor the miracle of life, and all that that means. We share hugs and stories. We laugh, cry, and pat each other on the back. No one is trying to impress anyone or convert anyone; these are some of the most honest, least pushy people I've ever met.

As for myself, presiding over IANDS meetings is my chance—most likely the only chance I'll ever have—to indulge my secret persona as a stand-up comic. Put a microphone in my hand and a receptive audience, and you'd have to seal my mouth with duct tape to keep me from spouting one-liners. I love connecting with people—talking to them, listening to them, drawing them out of their shells, making them laugh. During dark and stressful times, an IANDS gathering not only brightens my day but my whole outlook on life. It helps me to truly live the words of that old gospel hymn: "This little light of mine, I'm gonna let it shine. Let it shine, let it shine, let it shine."

CHAPTER TEN

MR. RIGHT

▼

Back in August of 1981, I had a dream. It went like this: I was standing alone in the living room while my house-mate, Christy, busied herself elsewhere in our house. I yelled out loudly to her, "When am I going to meet Mr. Right?" There was a knock at the front door. I opened it to find a man standing on the porch in the darkness. "You need to replace the bulb in your porch light," he said.

Fast-forward to June 1982. By then, I had bought Christy's share in the house and she was moving to her own place. A cadre of burly, willing paramedics from Seattle's elite Medic One corps was helping us move her things. Before their arrival, for some reason I decided to change the long-burned-out light bulb on the front porch. I pulled out a rickety chair, climbed up on it, and proceeded to dismantle the antique light fixture and replace the bulb. I was screwing the fixture back on, using my fingernail as a screwdriver, when the itty bitty screws slipped out of my hand, hit the porch, and rolled out of sight.

Now what? The thin metal fixture dangled by a single screw; if I let go, it would fall to the porch and break. But try as I might, I couldn't unfasten that screw with my fingernail. Meanwhile, my arm was going numb holding the fixture aloft in a Statue-of-

Liberty pose. As I pondered my dilemma, a wad of freshly chewed gum appeared right in front of my face. "Here," a voice said. "Use this." I mashed the soft gum to the rim of the light fixture to cement it in place; it held like a charm. Only then did I look down to see who my savior was.

I found myself gazing into the big, friendly face of my future husband, Don Sharp. I took note of clear blue-green eyes, straight dark-blond hair, high Slavic cheekbones, and a mustache framing an expressive mouth. He had a firefighter's powerful body and the gentle, protective demeanor of a golden retriever. Despite my prescient dream of the year before, I had not the slightest inkling that this was the man I would someday marry. So much for my vaunted mystical awareness and ability to sense the future.

Still, Don was a nice guy—I *could* see that. He had found his true calling when he joined the Seattle Fire Department ten years earlier. Like all the paramedics in the department's nationally recognized emergency medical service, he was a bit of a wild man and a prankster—traits that seem to be self-selecting for jobs that involve racing around at high speeds and saving people's lives under challenging conditions. The Medic One guys were on the street doing the down-and-dirty work that enabled me, a few hours later, to breeze in as an angel of mercy in the comfort of a sanitized hospital environment. They were men of action, like cowboys; I admired them beyond words. But romance? No, thanks. They were way too crazy—even for me.

It was only natural that Don and I would hang out with the same people, though, and we became friends. He seemed to be a kind person and a consummate volunteer on his time off. If anybody needed a helping hand, Don was the first one to provide it. He took care of people. Several times when a group of us had gone to the movies and were greeted by pouring rain upon leaving the theater, it was always Don who ran to get the car while the rest of us stayed dry under the marquee. He had an old-fashioned gallantry, doing the little things for women that most men didn't bother with anymore: holding car doors open, walking on the curb side, grabbing the check at a restaurant even when the relationship with his female companion was strictly platonic.

Perhaps what caught my eye most was his devotion to his two small children. Though divorced from their mom, he stayed very involved in their lives, and was so proud of them he'd use any excuse to whip out his wallet and show off their pictures. Since my own biological clock was beginning to tick rather noisily, this attribute was high on my list of desirable male virtues. But as far as envisioning Don and me as a couple, I just didn't get it.

Until our first date, that is. Of course, it wasn't a typical "date"—unless you consider ten days in a tropical paradise typical. With studied casualness, Don had asked me if I'd join him and some other friends for a spring vacation at his time-share condo in Maui. "A whole bunch of people are going to be there," he practically yawned. "We'll just party, get tan, and see who we can meet on the beach." The opportunity to escape Seattle's April monsoons sounded like a great idea, so I said yes.

Don met me at the airport in Maui and slipped a welcoming lei around my neck. He'd gotten a head start on his tan, and I couldn't help but notice that his muscular bare legs, which I'd never seen before, looked fabulous in shorts. Then he gave me an aloha kiss—a quick one at that—but somehow it turned everything around for me. In a flash of recognition, I knew this man. I mean I really *knew* him, at a level that transcended our jobs, our mutual friends, our social relationship, and the flesh and bone of how we normally presented ourselves to each other. The scales had fallen from my eyes.

In my youth, I'd entertained many romantic notions about finding a lifetime soul mate, but as I grew older and wiser, I decided those were the stuff of movies and pulp fiction. Whenever the subject of marriage came up, my standard comment was: "I'm meant to serve mankind, not one man." Yet as I sat next to Don in the rental car on the way to his condo, I felt certain I had indeed met my soul mate. It went beyond romance or sex, although that was part of it. It just seemed *right*. For fifteen years, my mother had prayed before every meal that I would meet and marry the mate God chose for me. Now, sneaking sidelong glances at Don while checking out the scenery, I dared to believe that her prayer—and mine—had finally been answered. This was Mr. Right.

"You're sure awfully quiet," said Don, interrupting my reverie. Like all my friends, Don was used to me being perky, not pensive. His words splashed cold water on my fevered imagination. *Whoa, Kim. Get a grip. Don asked you here as a friend, not a lover.* There was no quicker way to louse up a nice friendship—not to mention an expensive vacation—than by trying to inflate this relationship into something it's not. Specifically, a bigtime romance. So I told myself to cool it.

At the condo, I took the fold-down couch in the living room and Don got the bedroom. Everything was on the up-and-up, except there was no sign of any other guests. "Oh, they'll be along later," he said vaguely. For the next few days, we proceeded to behave in a perfectly respectable fashion: walking on the beach, sunbathing, noshing, shopping, sightseeing. Lots of conversation punctuated by long, awkward pauses. We pretended not to see the romantic couples we saw everywhere, entwined in each other's arms. When we had occasion to touch, we practically jumped back as if shocked by static electricity. I blamed myself for the tension between us, thinking I must have gotten addled by the seductive spell of the tropics.

On the third night, while we walked on the beach, I asked Don what had happened to all his friends who were supposed to be with us. He was quiet for a moment. Then he said, "I didn't invite anyone else."

"What? Excuse me?"

"I didn't invite anyone else," he said, with a note of defiance in his voice.

"Why not?"

"Because I was afraid that if I told you I wanted to take you out on our first date for ten days in Maui, you'd think I was nuts, and you would have said no." Indeed, he was probably right.

"This is a date?" I asked, incredulously.

"Well, I kind of thought it would be," said Don, looking miserable now. "But to tell you the truth, I think I'm just wrecking a good friendship, or at least the potential for a better friendship, by having romantic feelings for you." There, he'd said it. He felt the same way I did.

Engaged in small talk, we walked a little farther and then turned around and headed back to the condominium. When we were once again in front of the stone wall that held back the grasses of the condominium lawn, we began to talk more intimately.

"I want to tell you something that's going to sound a little crazy," Don said. "I don't think I'm going to survive getting off this island." Without any form of visible reaction I said, "That's very interesting, because I don't think I'm going to survive the trip home." We looked at each other without saying anything else. I had met someone who suddenly seemed to understand me so deeply that a strong and normal reaction was unnecessary. It's odd to look back and think that such conversation-eliciting comments did not spawn sharing that would have continued on through the night, but it didn't. It was as if we both knew that the other was telling the truth and nothing more needed to be said about it.

"So, I guess this is God's honeymoon to us," I said. "I had the same thought," Don said as he then turned to me, this time intending to get the kiss he'd been waiting for. He cupped my face in his hands and turned my lips to meet his. In the darkness I could see his face coming closer to mine and then I felt his warm breath against my mouth. Our lips were within microns of touching when, *slap*, something hard hit us and knocked us onto our backs in opposite directions. What the heck?! We both looked up in shock and then burst out into hysterical laughter.

At the very moment of our long-awaited kiss, the condominium lawn sprinklers came on. The sprinkler directly in front of us, instead of making the normal arcing half-circle of spray, shot a steady, hydrant-force stream of water to the exact point where our lips were about to meet. It hit us with such force that it literally knocked us off our feet. The timing was unbelievable, but our laughter had taken away the tension that we had felt. We knew that we were meant to kiss, but we reached an unspoken agreement that now was not the time. Laughing, sometimes so hard that we had to stop walking, we returned to the condo.

The next day, Don and I had a picnic on a sugar-sand beach in a gorgeous, secluded cove on the road to Hana. Somehow we missed a sign, clearly posted, that prohibited swimming because of dangerous currents. The water was clear and lovely and the waves quite tame. After we ate, Don decided to teach me how to bodysurf. I'm not a strong swimmer—OK, I hardly swim at all—but Don was a good teacher, showing me how to turn my back to the waves and let them gently carry me back to the beach. It was fun, and I kept following him farther and farther out. Soon,

I'd had enough. We agreed to quit after we caught the next big wave and rode it in to the beach.

But that wave carried us off to the side and away from land. The small waves we'd been riding turned to giant swells, and we began to rise and fall like little corks on the water, unable to touch bottom or paddle against the strong current that sucked us in every direction except the right one. I lost sight of Don as he dropped into a trough of water that appeared out of nowhere, and a wave broke over him. He popped up again, sputtering, and reached out with his strong arms to steady me as we tossed on the waves. We were drifting farther away from the beach, and I felt the first twinges of panic.

Then, off to the right, we heard the shrill cry of someone else in even more trouble: "Help! Help! I'm drowning!" The waves were so high we couldn't see him, but the voice was very close. Instantly, Don went into his Medic One mode. With energy from an adrenaline rush, he gave me a powerful shove toward the beach, then began stroking toward the screaming swimmer, who was struggling to stay afloat a few yards away. Unbeknown to us, the man had seen Don and me bodysurfing, decided to try it himself, and was carried out by the same current that had caught us.

As soon as Don left my side, a wave pulled me under the water and pushed me facedown into the sandy bottom. I couldn't lift my head against the force of the current. I held my breath as long as I could, but then came the inevitable expulsion of air and inhalation of water, grit, and tiny sea creatures, which entered my body like fire. I wasn't afraid, exactly; all my energy was focused on surviving. I really, really wanted to get out of the water. The next blast of current pulled my arms over my head, where I touched something big, solid, and very rough-textured. I grabbed hold for dear life, brought my head to the surface, and saw I had clutched a lava outcropping that extended out from the beach. Don had pushed me toward it. Dragging the upper portion of my body up on the coarse rock surface, which felt like it was embedded with broken Coke bottles, I threw up again and again. The waves nearly washed me off the rock, but nothing would make me let go. Painfully, I made my way over the lava to the beach and retched some more.

A very skinny, sweaty man ran up to me, a look of concern on his face. A marathon runner, he had been out on a training run when he saw me struggling in the water. Together, we peered into the vast expanse of sea, looking for Don. "See! There he is! Way out there!" the man said excitedly. Sure enough, far beyond the breaking surf, two tiny heads were visible. My heart caught in my throat. They were so far away and so tired. They needed help, but how could anyone reach them in time?

I climbed up on the highest point in the cove, a cluster of smooth rocks piled against an embankment, so I could have the best possible view. In my mind I formed a prayer, the most urgent I could remember. I called on God to send whatever angels or beings he could to save Don's life, a brave man who was risking his own life to save a stranger's. The prayer took on a shape and substance; I could see it in the same way that I saw angels. It stretched out long and tubular, somewhat like a tunnel, but filled with light, a light that seemed to emanate from my chest. I had never seen a prayer before. It flung itself out like a lifeline from my heart to the place where Don and the other man bobbed in the water.

In the next instant, I saw two objects speeding toward them. They looked like some sort of small motorized craft. As I squinted into the distance, I heard, to my horror, another cry for help. It was the runner! In a misguided display of overconfidence, he had gone into the water in a rescue attempt, gotten caught in the current, and now needed help himself. Wonderful. I was watching three men drown. Except for the power of prayer, I was helpless to save them. The churning water seemed to swallow everyone up. I stood alone on the rocks, searching waves as big as houses and straining my ears for the sound of cries for help. But there was nothing out there.

Suddenly, everyone appeared at once between the waves. The little motor boats I thought I'd seen were in fact surfboards, being paddled at amazing speeds by two broad-shouldered surfers. The first man to almost drown was thrown across one board, like a saddlebag, and the exhausted runner lay across another. Don trailed along behind, hanging on to the back of a surfboard.

The surfers skimmed their boards neatly through the pounding surf to the beach, then unloaded the three rescued men on the shore. The half-drowned men lay gasping and shivering on the sand. I was wrapping them in our towels and picnic blanket when a heavyset Hawaiian woman appeared, striding purposefully out of the jungle beside the beach. She wore a faded sarong and her thick black hair hung in a shank down her back. She wasn't just large, she was massive, and when she padded across the sand in her rubber-soled thongs, I swear the earth shook.

Her face was impassive as she headed straight for Don, who stood up at her approach. Slowly, she lifted her two huge brown arms, placed her hands on Don's shoulders, looked deep into his eyes and said, "You lucky, mon. No surfboarders, you dead. You lucky, mon." Her pronouncement concluded, she regally walked back into the jungle, while we watched in open-mouthed amazement.

I turned to thank the surfers for their rescue mission, but they were gone. Neither Don nor the other two men they'd fished out of the water saw them leave. No one knew their names or where they had come from or how they had happened to spot the drowning men. They simply vanished, like Tonto and the Lone Ranger. Definitely a woo-woo event, I thought. The men, however, saw nothing particularly strange about the timely appearance—and subsequent disappearance—of their rescuers. "Oh, they must have surfed off in search of another cove," said Don. But I knew who the surfers really were, and who had sent them. Never, never underestimate the power of prayer.

The rest of our vacation wasn't quite as dramatic, thank goodness. To make a long story shorter, we fell in love. By the time I left Maui five days later, Don and I were acting like honeymooners. We had a ball doing all the cornball tourist activities, and I discovered Don had a hambone almost as big as mine. When we attended a luau at a resort hotel, the staff picked the barrel-chested Don to dress up in a wig, grass skirt, and coconut-shell bra. He vamped so energetically, he brought the house down.

I loved Don's humor and optimistic spirit. He never entered a room without whistling, and he didn't let anything get him down for long. "Hey, the worst day I ever had was great," he would say. We had the same midwestern values and even said the same Lutheran prayer at mealtime: "Come, Lord Jesus, be our guest. Let these gifts to us be blessed." I had never known a man who prayed with me. Nor had I known a man on whom I felt I could depend utterly, completely. Though I had loved George, he was not such a man. Don was.

A particular morning is lodged forever in my memory. I was groggy with sleep, my eyes still closed, as my senses began to awake. The ceiling fan swished above me and the early morning breeze was heavy with the almost overpowering fragrance of plumeria blossoms. I could hear the unfamiliar songs of island birds, and the more familiar sounds of bacon sizzling and coffee being brewed. I slowly opened my eyes to the welcome sight of Don whistling happily as he made breakfast in the kitchen. I made a mental note to myself to always remember this moment, so I would be sure to reexperience it upon my death. This wasn't a morbid thought, but a practical one. Though I didn't have a life review during my near-death experience—in which scenes from one's life click through one's consciousness with the speed and clarity of a slide show—I fully expect to make up for that omission when I die, and it's going to be a doozy. So I often take occasions such as that gorgeous morning with Don in the kitchen and freeze-frame them in my memory to they'll be there when I need them.

The night before I left Maui, the weather was unsettled and so was I. Something was on my mind and I couldn't sleep. In the wee hours of the morning, I slipped outside the sliding-glass door and stood on the lanai as the wind from a tropical disturbance whipped around me. Storm clouds scuttled across the dark sky. It was a month before my thirty-fifth birthday, which I had foreseen in my near-death experience that I would not live to celebrate. In only a few hours, I would be getting on a plane for Seattle, and I had foreseen I would die in the crash of a small white plane. Only a month earlier, I had been on a commuter flight from Spokane that was struck by lightning. A case could be made that I was tempting fate, and my family and friends had expressed concern about my cavalier attitude with regard to my premonition. If it happens, it happens, I told them. After all, I had no fear of death. It meant a reunion with God, my Creator, and the people I loved who'd already died.

But this honeymoon in Maui had changed that attitude. I wasn't ready to leave this world—not now. I wasn't ready to leave Don, or to forgo the future I hoped we would share. The wind blew my hair around my face as I sent a prayer up into the restless clouds. "Dear God," I said, "I want to live. I want to be with this man. Give me my life. I pray in the name of Jesus. Amen." I stepped back inside the condo, where Don lay sleeping. In a few minutes, I was asleep, too.

Morning dawned clear, calm, and beautiful. But by the time I was ready to board my plane at the airport, the sky had turned stormy again. I barely took notice, so busy was I talking with Don. After one last hug, I walked out on the tarmac with my fellow passengers. I nearly stopped in my tracks when I saw what was waiting for us: a small white plane. As if ordered by a heavenly stage manager, the dark boiling clouds momentarily parted and a beam of sunlight shone right down on the plane, making it look even whiter. Nice special effects. All we needed now were trumpets and a drumroll.

I was walking toward the plane when someone grabbed my wrist and turned me around. It was Don. He had pushed past the airline personnel at the gate and had run out on the tarmac to catch me. Over the noise of the wind and the planes, he shouted, "I love you!" It was the first time he'd said those words to me. "I love you, too!" I shouted back. "Thanks for the honeymoon!"

The plane ride to Honolulu was one of the roughest of my life. The storm shut down the Maui airport right after we took off. We were tossed around like a cat might toss a toy in the air, bouncing up and down as we hit one air pocket after another. Passengers were crying. They clutched barf bags. They grabbed their armrests and said prayers. When they called for a flight attendant, no one came. Moving around the plane was so unsafe that the attendants stayed buckled in their seats.

Through it all, I sat calmly with a big silly grin on my face. I was happy because I wasn't afraid. I was probably the only person in the cabin who was absolutely convinced that we would land safely in Honolulu, which we did. I knew I would make my connecting flight to Seattle; that Don would return in a few days, and we would be in each other's arms again. God had given me life and he had given me Don, and I wasn't about to lose either one anytime soon.

My near-death experience had taught me many things over the years, and one of the most important was the power I have—that we all have—to make our own choices. My visions, powerful as they seemed, were like maps. They revealed potential courses or directions for my life, but they did not force a certain route upon me. They did not command my future. It was still me standing at the fork in the road, still me making the choice—left or right. This way or that. I was making such a choice now. Again, I wanted to live.

CHAPTER ELEVEN

THE NEAR-DEATH EXPERIENCE QUILT

▼

D ON AND I GOT IT BACKWARD. We started off with a honeymoon—then we began a courtship that took three more years to result in marriage. Don is a wonderful husband, but he was a reluctant groom. During our lengthy, sometimes maddening, journey to the altar, I learned a great deal about the value of patience—never my strong suit—and perseverance.

I talk a lot about lessons and how they advance our spiritual maturity, but the truth is, I hate them. Learning isn't an easy process; in fact, it's often very painful. I have to work through the pain in much the same way as a woman going through natural childbirth: Breathe through it, try to stay focused, and emerge with something truly wonderful when it's over. Spiritual growth is usually the reward at the end of my lessons, but that still doesn't make me like them. If I had designed our earthly curriculum, we'd have more snap courses and a lot less pain.

Though my love life was frustrating, my career was going great guns. With my colleague Michael Boltwood, I coauthored a chapter for the new edition of Mosby's Comprehensive Review of Critical Care—a well-thumbed volume which was the basic handbook for nurses working the critical care unit. Our particular chapter, the psychosocial aspects of critical care, explained how patients are affected by various aspects of the high-tech, intensive care environment—loss of privacy, sensory overload, painful procedures, etc.—and how to make treatment as humane as possible under dehumanizing conditions. For the most part, I covered problems that were familiar to nursing staff, such as weaning a patient from a ventilator, or breaking the news of a patient's death to family members.

Then I ventured into unfamiliar territory, at least as far as traditionalists were concerned. I discussed what constitutes a near-death experience, and how to respond to a patient who's had one. I held my breath when we sent off the manuscript, afraid that this unorthodox information would never survive the editor's scrutiny. But when the galleys came back, there it was, every single word. To my knowledge, it marks the first examination of the near-death experience within the pages of a medical textbook.

Another first was the publication of the protocol I developed for treatment of near-death experiencers. Through my work at Harborview, my independent research, and personal experience, I devised some simple strategies—in the clinical field we call them interventions—for nurses and other hospital caregivers to use following a medical emergency in which a near-death experience occurs. They formed the basis for a chapter I contributed to *The Near-Death Experience: Problems, Prospects, Perspectives*, edited by (then) University of Michigan psychiatrist Bruce Greyson and Miami University sociologist Charles Flynn. At the time it was published a decade ago, this book represented the most exhaustive examination of near-death studies to date. It featured writings by prominent scholarly researchers and theoreticians from Kenneth Ring to Carl Sagan, who debated the biomedical, psychological, and philosophical explanations for the near-death phenomenon. I was thrilled to be in such distinguished company.

My concerns as a social worker, however, were less intellectual and more practical. Such as: How do you help reorient patients to their surroundings following an "other-world" experience? How do you assure them they are sane and normal? How do you help them get on with their lives? How do you deal with their family members, and their worries about their loved ones' apparent changes in behavior or personality?

Medical professionals have the opportunity to help bring near-death experiencers down to earth, so to speak, and reorient them even before their heart resumes beating again or before they regain consciousness. The technique is simple but effective. This is how I described it in *The Near-Death Experience:*

> One of the things I train clinicians to do . . . is to orient the patient to time, to place, and to who they are, using their name as well as conversing with the patient and letting him or her know what is going on with his or her body at that time. I also suggest that staff assure them they are being taken care of. Some staff people find it comfortable to do this. For those who feel awkward verbalizing all of this in front of their coworkers, I suggest that they *think* it. Even though a staff person may not verbally communicate, subtle nonverbal communication is sometimes possible during an NDE.

Anecdotal evidence suggests that some people who appear unconscious, even lifeless, are nevertheless acutely aware of the thoughts and feelings of those around them. (It happened to me.) So if the clinician is uncomfortable saying out loud to a person in cardiac arrest, "Mrs. Smith, this is Seattle, and it's Wednesday morning, May 24, 1995," the mere *thinking* of such a message might also convey the necessary information to the patient.

Once the patient has been successfully resuscitated—even before it's known whether an NDE occurred—I recommend that a nurse or physician help reestablish body awareness by lightly touching the patient's body.

The staff member simply outlines, with his or her hands, the patient's body, starting with the head and moving down the sides. The rationale for this is that if they have been out of the body, they may need to be reoriented to their body boundaries . . . By outlining the patient's body, we can get the patient adjusted to being back in the body again. It should be a light touch quickly done, like frisking a person at an airport, and does not involve much pressure, nor does it have to be obvious to others in the room.

What near-death experiencers seek above all else is validation of what they've been through. My mantra always began with words to this effect: "I want you to know that what happened to you was real." To have it dismissed as a dream or a side effect of drug treatment or the hallucinatory response of a traumatized brain not only denies the spiritual or mystical nature of their experience but also trivializes its significance. It contradicts what they know in their gut to be true. This sets up a dissonance that may take years to resolve.

While I encourage health care professionals to elicit comments from patients about any perceptions or memories they may have had during the time they were unconscious, it's important to remember that the most common response to an NDE is none at all. Some people want to talk about their near-death experience as soon as they are able. But most either are not ready to deal with it, or do not remember it until much later. At Harbor-

view, I frequently did not hear about a near-death experience
until after the patient was discharged from the hospital and had
returned for a follow-up clinic visit.

Instead of being happy at having been resuscitated, many
people paradoxically respond with deep sadness. They are grieving the separation from the most enlightening and transforming
experience of their lives. Despite their renewed love and appreciation for life in this world, the sadness lingers—at least for a
while. For some, the sense of loss is overwhelming. At Harborview, I looked into one tear-stained face after another and I saw
myself and the tears I had shed for weeks after I was revived in
Shawnee Mission.

The grief may be exacerbated if the near-death experiencer
is reunited with, and then forced to leave, loved ones who have
already died. This was the case with Lani Leary Houck, whose
mother had been the most important person in her life. Lani had
often thought of things to tell her mother if she could just see
her one more time. When Lani was reunited with her mom during
her near-death experience, it was like a dream come true, as well
as an opportunity for healing and closure. However, she was dev-
astated at having to leave the Light. She recalled,

To me that Light doesn't need a word. So if someone
needs to call it Buddha or Jesus or God, I would say "yes,"
but for me, it was love. I knew that I was forgiven for
anything and everything. I was loved and I knew that
would never, ever change. *Bliss* is a word that doesn't
even come close to describing that moment. So when I
heard a communication to me that said, "You have to go
back," I screamed, *"No!"* right from the center of my
being. I couldn't and still can't imagine leaving the pres-

ence of that love and light. I have a lot of moments of wanting to go Home, and of feeling very, very lonely.

For Gene Baker, encountering a number of deceased relatives during his near-death experience—many of whom had died before his birth—was the most healing moment of love he had ever experienced. They commiserated with him about their knowledge that the next few years of his life would be difficult ones, with no easy way out. They also told Gene he had to return to this world so he could continue to learn and to give.

Anger often goes hand in hand with sadness, and for years, Gene was angry with the relatives he had met on the other side, believing it was their fault he had to return to his body and to the hardships he faced in this world. Nevertheless, I have seen the adage "Time heals all wounds" borne out again and again in the lives of near-death experiencers, and so it was with Gene. His anger gradually melted away and he realized that life in this world could actually be more wonderful than he had expected. Today, he reaches out to others who are struggling with depression, to reassure them that change can come and life can be better.

Another common reaction to the near-death experience is excitement or agitation that leads to precipitous life change. In a case similar to the affluent lawyer who proposed living among street people, one woman wanted to give away all her possessions because she no longer valued material things. My standard counsel is to discourage *everyone* from making hasty, drastic decisions as a result of a near-death experience. Besides, there are usually other stressors in their lives related to the underlying illness or accident that caused them to be clinically near death that may mandate lifestyle changes anyway. Worried families should be reassured that their patience and support will help the near-death experiencer integrate the experience into his or her life without having to turn everything upside down.

However, the bottom line is there's no predicting how patients or their family members will respond initially. It helps to educate them as much as possible about near-death phenomena, even to the extent of assigning them research. That was certainly the case with the wife of Mr. Jones, a forty-three-year-old attorney who survived ventricular fibrillation and began talking about his near-death experience as soon as the oxygen tube was removed from his throat. He described leaving his body, entering a tunnel, and seeing beautiful, radiant light. But when his wife showed up in the coronary care unit, Mr. Jones said nothing about these unusual events.

Mrs. Jones chatted at length with the nurse about her and her husband's careers as successful attorneys, their desire to start a family soon, and the patient's avocation as a mountain climber. The evening-shift nurse reported that Mrs. Jones left the hospital at dinnertime but later returned with a number of books on coronary disease. She proceeded to read excerpts to Mr. Jones from the books about impending diet changes, medicines, and the necessity for low-level activities. Mr. Jones lay silently until his wife told him about her plans to take a CPR (cardiopulmonary resuscitation) course. He blew up and yelled, "I was in the most beautiful place imaginable and then yanked back to find myself stuffed in the throat, pinned to a bed, and forced to hear this (expletive deleted) crap! I'd rather be dead! Don't you dare use CPR on me!" The couple had a huge fight, during which Mr. Jones threw several PVCs (premature ventricular contractions). Convinced by the nurse that the patient was dangerously stressed, Mrs. Jones left his room . . . Mr. Jones was sedated by the physician.

Mr. Jones didn't want to talk about his future health or anything else except his NDE, and his wife felt threatened by this attitude. Since her coping mechanism was to intellectualize, as evidenced by her use of books on cardiac disease, I sent her to the library to look up everything she could find on near-death experiences. This gave her a task not centered on her husband, and it satisfied her need to research matters on her own. The upshot of all this was she learned a great deal and became more understanding of what her husband had gone through. Eventually, they were able to resolve their disagreement.

One category for which clinical intervention has not been developed is that of the frightening near-death experience. For a long time, I thought there was no such thing. Then I met Cindy, a fourteen-year-old girl who had been raped and strangled and was admitted to the intensive care unit with respiratory problems resulting from the strangulation. With a look of tremendous fear on her face, she resisted all efforts to sedate her, which was necessary in order to put a ventilator tube down her throat. We assumed her reaction was due to the violence she had suffered. But when the tube was removed and she could talk again, she told me of her terrifying encounter with Satan.

I was so thunderstruck by her story that I reacted exactly the way I had with Maria: I doubted her. And in trying to lighten the mood, I made an offhand remark that I have regretted ever since. "How did you know it was Satan?" I asked. "Did he present his card?" How could I, of all people, have sounded so patronizing? I was filled with self-recrimination. And I couldn't explain why I found her account so hard to believe—even though I had gone one-on-one with a demon myself. It just wasn't the way near-death experiences were supposed to be, I thought. Yet this girl had the same undeniable sincerity that I had seen in other near-death experiencers. Eventually, I had to conclude that if her experience wasn't real, neither was mine. I had to accept the fact that some near-death experiences were filled not with love and light but terror and despair.

The reality of dark, sometimes "hellish" experiences was discounted even by the founders of IANDS. The possibility that we could leave our bodies when we were close to death and experience a joyous reunion with God and/or loved ones was acceptable. The opposite was not. Ironically, the very reasons used to debunk heavenly experiences—such as attributing them to hallucinations or drug reactions—were used by the early NDE explorers to reject the possibility of frightening experiences.

But to those who have had one, its reality is beyond question. In fact, these experiencers describe what they endured in very similar terms as those used to describe a heavenly experience, saying that what happened to them was *more* real than the three-dimensional world we think of as reality. And just like those who have a rapturous NDE, they find that they are profoundly changed afterward. For example, most of the people I'm aware of who've had frightening NDEs—at least those who describe themselves as Christians—have become more fundamentalist and Bible-based in their religion.

Steve Huseby's life became a spiritual roller coaster ride after his terrifying near-death experience. While serving in Vietnam as a military policeman, Steve was nearly killed by a hand-grenade explosion. At the hospital, his heart stopped and Steve next found himself being carried along by two beings, one on either side of him, toward the gates of Hell. The walls were built from what looked like large black blocks, outlined in red light; the overall impression was of a place that absorbed light rather than giving it off. From somewhere, Steve heard a booming voice say, "This one has not yet fulfilled my purpose," and he found himself back in his body.

Steve was so affected by this unsettling experience that he concluded the Protestant religion of his childhood was insufficient to encompass the spiritual world he now knew coexisted with the secular one. In an attempt to delve deeper into what he perceived as the greater reality—good and evil, heaven and hell—he experimented with black magic and the occult. Then came another reversal, as he spent two years in a missionary Baptist seminary studying to become a preacher. Though he eventually decided not to enter the ministry, he still finds the Bible his most important source of spiritual inspiration.

In two important cases, both near-death experiencers told me they felt that what happened to them needed to take place in order to bring about necessary life changes.

Howard Storm was chairman of the art department at Northern Kentucky University and was leading an art tour for college students in Paris when he was hospitalized with a perforated duodenum. The pain became so great that Howard left his body and observed it lying in bed, his wife seated next to him. Unable to get her attention, he followed some beings who looked like humans, beckoning to him. He followed them into a foggy realm that grew progressively darker. Then they revealed themselves as demonic beings who attacked him. To his surprise, Howard discovered that saying words with religious implications, such as *God* would frighten the creatures away. Alone in the darkness and in despair, he cried out, "Jesus, please save me!" Such an exhortation was unlike Howard, who described himself as a resolute atheist, someone who believed that he, not God, was the center of the universe.

As soon as Howard called out for help, a Light came down from above, lifting him up. Howard's experience then took on the nature of a positive near-death experience. He found himself surrounded by loving spiritual beings and saw a review of his life, which he observed had been almost entirely self-serving. He was appalled. Yet he felt no condemnation from the beings around him. A question-and-answer session then followed, something that also occasionally happens in heavenly NDEs, and all of the questions Howard could think to ask were answered fully.

Upon his recovery, Howard was convinced that his near-death experience had served to put him in a position of helplessness for the first time in his life, forcing him to seek God's help. Today, he is a minister of a church in Cincinnati. "If there is any one lesson I would share from this, it would be that we are put here in this world to love one another," he says.

Steven Westman may not have been as egocentric as Howard Storm, but he lived and worked in a godless world, as a thief and drug dealer in the Seattle area. While drunk one evening, Steven was hit by a car and was in a coma for ten days. During that time, Steven found himself in what he insists was Hell, a place where he had no control over his life, where Satan told him to do things and he did them. Eventually, Steven found himself returning to earth. As the planet loomed closer, Steven was terrified by the thought that he was returning as a kind of puppet agent for Satan. He was shown his life, from infancy up through the accident that had landed him in the hospital. Then he found his movement toward earth slowing, and reversing. Planets receded as he moved back out into space.

"Why did I choose to live the way I did?" Steven found himself asking. Off in the distance, a pinpoint of light grew larger and he suddenly found himself before Christ, who said, "Welcome, son. Tell me how you've lived your life." Steven began talking, but when he came to a time in his life he was ashamed of, he tried to lie about it. He also realized that Christ knew all about it anyway. "Tell me the truth of how you've lived your life," he heard again. Steven complied. Then he returned to his body, shocked and humbled.

According to his father, who spent several months by his bedside while Steven recovered, the first word his son uttered when he awoke from his coma was, "Incredible." His first discernible sentence was, "Read the big book." He now works as a landscape gardener for a church, and is unequivocal in his belief that his near-death experience was directly related to the kind of life he had been living beforehand.

Complicating the process of explaining the tremendous variety of near-death experiences is the fact that only a minority actually involve an encounter with the Light. I have talked with a sizable percentage of near-death experiencers who have had tremendous awareness of love, forgiveness, and knowledge, but whose experience occurred entirely in darkness. Based on my interviews of well over a thousand near-death experiencers, only about 30 percent involved the Light. The presence or absence of light does not seem to be the determining factor about whether an experience is spiritually positive or negative.

Nancy Evans Bush, who has a master's degree in pastoral ministry and is the current president of IANDS, was in her early twenties and in her second pregnancy when she went into premature labor. Her blood pressure suddenly dropped and she lost consciousness. In a journal, she explained:

I was aware not of the flurry around me but of moving rapidly upward into darkness. Although I don't recall turning to look, I knew the hospital and the world were receding below me very fast . . . I was rocketing through space like an astronaut without a capsule. A small group of circles appeared ahead of me toward the left. To the right was just a dark space. The circles were black and white and made a clicking sound as they snapped black to white, white to black. They were jeering and tormenting—not evil, exactly, but more mocking and mechanistic. The message in their clicking was: Your life never existed, the world never existed, your family never existed. You were allowed to make it up. It was never there. There was never anything there. That's the joke— it was all a joke. There was much laughter on their parts, malicious laughter. It was empty except for me and them and dark. Not like night dark; somehow it was thinner, whatever that means . . . it just seemed to go on forever.

In this awful emptiness, Nancy remembered trying frantically to prove the reality of her existence by recalling details of her mother's life, things she knew about her mother's childhood in another part of the country. "How could I have made that up? And my first baby—I knew her. I knew I hadn't made her up. And childbirth—why would I have ever made up that? I was trying to summon up some strong memory of my husband and the house. Something tangible to argue with." Her arguments were to no avail.

They just kept jeering: "This is eternity." This is all there ever was and all there will ever be—just this despair. That utter emptiness just went on and on, and they kept on clicking. The grief was wrenching. This world gone and grass and hills and my first baby and all the other babies . . . I knew that no one could bear that much grief, but there didn't seem to be any end of it and no way out. Everyone I loved was gone. Time was forever, endless. There's a cosmic terror (in that) that we have never addressed. The despair was because of the absolute conviction that I had seen what the other side was, and there was no way to tell anyone. It wouldn't matter how I died or when—damnation was out there just waiting.

Nancy and I had both come face-to-face with evil personified. For me, it had been a haunted house and a persistent demon; for Nancy, it was a near-death experience. It took Nancy twenty-five years to talk about it. People who've had frightening NDEs are even more reluctant to discuss them than those who've had pleasant ones. I call that reticence "fear of flakiness." Our culture tends to discount people who've had transformational experiences that cannot be observed, measured, or logically explained. Skepticism is an effective deterrent against baring one's soul. It's hard enough to testify about a wonderful and moving near-death experience; imagine the difficulty for those whose experience was hellish and terrible. They wonder what's "wrong" with them, what such an experience says about them. They often need a great deal of encouragement to come forward.

Dave Johnson confronted a terrifying beast during his near-death experience, but turned it into a loving encounter. A muscular general contractor—and a heavy drinker—Dave suffered a heart attack one day while he was pouring concrete. He was rushed to the hospital where he lay close to death for the next twenty-four hours. He felt himself leaving his body and passing at great speed through a tunnel toward an intensely bright light.

When he got to the light, he saw a dark, ugly, repellent creature standing to one side. Despite its frightening aspect, Dave felt compelled to hug it. Instantly, the beast was transformed into a brilliant shaft of light, opening onto a beautiful pastoral scene. There were people there, who seemed to be welcoming him. Dave felt warmer, more secure, and more loved than he had ever felt in his life—even with his wife and children, whom he loved dearly. But some power kept him from stepping forward into this new dimension. Before he knew it, Dave was accelerating back through the tunnel again, and returned to his own body.

Upon recovery, Dave found he'd lost his taste for alcohol. Without intervention but with the support of a huge network of friends and his family, he stopped drinking completely. He remains sober today.

There sometimes seems to be no rhyme or reason as to what sort of person has a gloomy near-death experience; I know a contemplative nun, a woman whose life is devoted to prayer and meditation, who had one. Even children can have them.

I once counseled a twelve-year-old girl who had been a patient at Children's Hospital and Medical Center in Seattle and was dying of a brain tumor. During one of her many medical crises, she'd lost consciousness and had seen a demonic beast that took on a human form. It had sharp teeth and nails and it clawed at her. This thing put her in a box that resembled a coffin, intending to keep her like a pet—or a prisoner. This girl was afraid of dying because this had been a terrifying experience for her.

The people around her at the time—all loving, caring people—tried to dismiss her experience as a bad dream. They said it might have been caused by the drugs she was taking or loss of blood or the tumor pressing on her brain, but whatever the cause, her "dream" didn't mean anything. They hoped this would reassure her and calm her, but it didn't. By contrast, the first thing

I told her was that what had happened to her was real. As we talked, she broke down and cried. She told me how scary death was to her, and how hard it was to be racing toward it. The doctors had given her only a few weeks to live. My advice was simple. I told her to pray—to talk to God just as if she were talking to her best friend—and ask God to take away the burden of her fear. She died just a few days later, much sooner than expected, but very much at peace, very serene. The fear was gone.

Where do frightening near-death experiences come from? I don't know why people who are "good," who have nothing to make amends for, have them. I think they are part of the dichotomy of light and dark, good and bad, yin and yang. The overwhelming preponderance of testimony from those who have approached the "other side" is that it is a place of unconditional love—where fear does not exist, where our past life can be seen with perfect awareness, and where broken connections with loved ones are joyfully made whole again. The hellish opposite would be where darkness and fear prevail, joy and love does not exist, nothing has meaning, and pain and suffering seem eternal.

By the time nine-year-old Cory Protzeller died of leukemia in 1985, he was well acquainted with both pain and paradise. He had known the pain since the age of three, when he was first diagnosed with leukemia and began the chemotherapy that would prolong—but ultimately would not save—his life. With the help of his family and physicians, he had fought off the disease again and again, only to suffer another relapse. He'd grown weary of the endless battle that his existence had become.

His illness had made him the focal point of his family's life, a fact of which he was acutely aware. When Elisabeth Kübler-Ross came to Seattle for a television appearance with terminally ill children and their siblings, Cory was given the guest-of-honor's seat: Elisabeth's lap. But for reasons none of us fully understood at first, Cory made a beeline for me instead. Then we realized Cory had done so in order to let his sister sit in Elisabeth's lap and be the center of attention for a change. That was Cory.

This little boy had learned that there was a special place waiting for him somewhere else—a place that contained more peace, joy, and tranquility than the disease-ravaged limitations of his life on earth. He called this place Summerland, and he drew beautiful pictures of it in vivid colors. After the first time he visited Summerland, he told his mother, "I'm not afraid to die. I have been to the crystal castle and have talked with God." He said he'd traveled up a tunnel of light to heaven, where he crossed over a rainbow bridge and saw the castle. God was there. He had engulfed Cory in loving light and told him not to worry, that he would not die yet, but it would happen soon. When it did, he would go to Summerland for good.

Cory met friends of his—other children who'd died of cancer—who were happy and carefree at Summerland. Illness and pain did not exist there. He was given to understand the time of his death had been set and nothing would change it. This did not frighten Cory because he was enjoying his visits to Summerland more and more. On Mother's Day, three months after sharing the television stage with his sister, after he and his family had agreed to decline further medical treatment, Cory took his last breath. In his mother's arms, Cory made his final trip to Summerland. At his funeral, everyone received a card on which was printed Cory's drawing of the rainbow bridge leading to the crystal castle.

Though Cory had lived half his life on the brink of death, Summerland did not appear in the form of near-death experiences per se, but in a series of visions that revealed what his future held.

Summerland became so fully integrated into his life that he could go there at will. Like a toddler on the playground who keeps running back to his mother for reassurance, Cory needed to be able to come and go until he was sure his family could handle the idea of his leaving for good.

Many things happen in childhood that become blurred with time or that we forget altogether—but not a near-death experience. The impact is lasting, and is remembered as vividly in adulthood as if it just occurred yesterday. Such was the case with Rick Bayley, who was a grown man when he became involved with Seattle IANDS ten years ago.

Rick nearly died when he was seven years old. He spiked a high fever—106 degrees—and was put into a bathtub filled with cool water to bring down his temperature. His sister, mother, and the family doctor were in the bathroom with him while his dad waited in the car to rush Rick to the hospital as soon as they lowered the fever a little. To his surprise, Rick found himself observing this scene through the eyes of his sister, who busied herself circulating water around his shivering body with her hand. He rose above it all, watching everything: his worried mother talking to the doctor, his anxious father in the car, the emergency room where he was taken, in a coma. (When Rick came to, he startled the attendants by demanding to know why they had left the curtain open on an observation window —a lapse which allowed a curious twelve-year-old girl to watch him being treated, thereby mortifying his out of-body self.)

During his coma, he entered a long tunnel or cave, watched a brief review of his life (at seven, there's not that much to review), and emerged at what he described as the mouth of the cave at the ocean. He remembered that he could play in the tunnel, stopping whenever he wanted to see, touch, smell, hear, and feel his surroundings. Outside the cave, he looked out over the water and saw a fine mist or thin layer of fog which obscured his view of the waterline. Rick knew that if he crossed the sea, he would not return. In the distance, he saw large storm clouds gathering, but felt safe and warmed by a bright, soothing light. He didn't know where the light came from; it was just there. While he was in the light, he felt a great deal of love and wisdom. At some point, beyond the reach of his adult memory, he returned to his body and awoke from his coma.

In my A-to-Z seminar on the near-death experience for health care workers, I spend a considerable amount of time discussing the various scientific explanations for what we call near-death phenomena. There are many, many theories. Carl Sagan has suggested that the tunnel effect is simply a mental reenactment of the birth process—our first, primitive memory, which is automatically triggered in the brain when we die. I once spoke to a group of obstetric/gynecological specialists from the University of Washington, and asked them what they thought of this idea. Their comments revealed a certain amount of skepticism.

For one, the doctors noted that the birth canal is a narrow, cramped place—the very opposite of the tunnel through which many travel in an NDE, which is invariably described as very expansive. The baby's head—indeed, its entire body—is crammed so tightly against the cervix that little or no light could enter. Some babies are born with their eyes squeezed shut; others with them open, but all newborns have great difficulty focusing on or even distinguishing objects in their visual field. They can barely tell the difference between light and dark. There's also the question of how this theory would apply to the numerous people who were born by Caesarean section, who've also had near-death experiences.

Other explanations include: hypoxia (lack of oxygen) or hypercarbnia (too much carbon dioxide); drug-induced hallucinations or dreams; and the release of B-endorphins in the brain. If you've ever seen someone suffering from oxygen deprivation, as I have, you know that they are befuddled, disoriented. Yet there is an almost preternatural clarity in the observations of near-death experiencers. Words may fail them, but they are *very* clear about what they've been through, how they perceived it, and the sequence of events.

As for drug-induced hallucinations, many near-death experiencers—especially those of my generation—know exactly what those feel like, and the NDE is markedly different. Besides, only one in five near-death experiencers are on any medication at all, and most such drugs are not hallucinogenic. When I was working the intensive care unit, heavy-duty medication actually seemed to interfere with my patients remembering a near-death experience. It didn't create or enhance the memory; it wiped it out.

The endorphin theory is related to the fact that when the body is stressed or in pain, it releases natural chemicals (B-endorphins) which kill the pain and can cause euphoric feelings. Physical exercise can trigger their release (the so-called runner's high); so can intense religious or creative experiences. I happen to be naturally well supplied with endorphins, so much so that I don't necessarily need novocaine when I get a tooth filled at the dentist—I can block out that kind of pain. Some researchers hypothesize that near-death experiences result when a flood of endorphins provoke hyperactivity within the brain's limbic system, the seat of our emotions. They argue that if the brain is wired so as to respond this way in times of extreme physical stress, that would explain the uniformity of the near-death experience among diverse cultural, racial, and religious populations. However, as Melvin Morse has written, there are no studies showing that the stress of dying produces large amounts of these chemicals, or that they can generate the unique and varied elements of a near-death experience.

I know a sociologist who can list the sociological reasons why near-death experiences occur. I know a theologian who can explain them theologically. Because we are humans with an innate urge to find reasons for the way things happen in our world, we want to explain things and categorize them. The near-death experience, though, cannot be so easily accounted for. I think it is its own thing. If you try to define it rationally, scientifically, and put it in a box, you can't do it. It evaporates.

Even Dr. Daniel Carr, an endocrinologist and leading promulgator of the limbic-lobe dysfunction theory, recognizes that clinical investigation of these matters can go only so far. "Even if careful scientific studies establish beyond any doubt the physiological substrate of dying, they would still have no relevance to the philosophic meaning of death, or its religious aspects," Carr writes in *The Near-Death Experience: Problems, Prospects, Perspectives.* The obvious parallel he draws is with the birth experience. "While studies of the mechanisms of birth have given rise to many advances in knowledge and therapy, metaphysical questions about the meaning of entering the world remain unanswerable by experimental science."

Perhaps Melvin Morse said it best in *Closer to the Light:*

Near-death experiences appear to be a cluster of events so that one cannot understand the total by looking at its various pieces. One cannot understand music by studying the various frequencies of sound that generate each note, nor does one need to have a deep understanding of acoustical physics to enjoy Mozart. The near-death experience remains a mystery.

CHAPTER TWELVE

ANGEL BABIES

▼

AS I BECAME increasingly absorbed in the study of near-death experiences, the occupational hazards of a high-stress work environment were taking their toll. I realized I was getting more satisfaction out of teaching, writing, lecturing, and supervising neophyte social workers than I got out of my day-to-day responsibilities at Harborview. We all chafed at the demands of the bureaucracy that had evolved to manage the complex operations of a large, publicly funded medical center. The more paperwork we fed the number crunchers, the more they wanted—and the less time was left over for patients. The "Zoo on the Hill" had been the professional and social center of my life for nearly ten years, but I was burned out. It was time for a change.

So I prepared to begin 1985 with a new job—as director of the newly created department of social work at Fred Hutchinson Cancer Research Center. The "Hutch," as it was called, was the first, largest, and most famous bone marrow transplant center in the world. Only a few blocks uptown from Harborview, it operated in a different social universe. The bill for a bone marrow transplant was a hundred thousand dollars and up—prepaid. Either insurance or private funds had to foot the bill. For once, I'd be working with a population of patients who consistently maintained checkbooks, had permanent mailing addresses, and even knew their own zip codes. The idea of a street person taking a leak in a hallway at Fred Hutchinson was unthinkable.

But as I cleaned out my desk at Harborview, I found myself overcome with affection for the hospital where I had found my true calling and earned my service stripes in social work. Good-bye, screaming ambulances. Good-bye, whackos, winos, and weirdos. Good-bye, caring hospital with such tremendous heart. Good-bye, bleary interns and gallows humor. What would I do without Harborview's daily installment of life-and-death drama? It was better than a soap opera. No doubt about it, I was going to miss the joint.

I wasn't the only one having trouble with change. Sally Dawson, the previous owner of my house, had come back. Not in the flesh this time, but in spirit. After she sold the house and moved to eastern Washington, Sally had made several trips back to Seattle with her friends. They always dropped by so Sally could show them the house on which she'd lavished so much love and attention. It had been her first house and it was hard for her to let go. I understood that; it was my first house, too. So I was always happy to accommodate her visits—her flesh-and-bone ones, that is.

But lately, Sally had taken to showing up in ghostly form. The first time this happened was on a quiet night when I was watching TV downstairs after my new housemate, Marsha Miller, had already gone to bed. Suddenly, I heard Marsha scream. Her feet hit the floor and she came running down the stairs. "Have you been here the whole time?" she asked me, wild-eyed.

"Yes," I said.

"You didn't crawl into bed with me?"

I laughed. "No, I'm quite sure, Marsha, that I did not crawl into bed with you."

"Well, something did." Marsha, an earthy, practical woman who also worked at Harborview and had zero tolerance for "woo-woos," was not the sort to imagine ghostly visitations. But something had obviously spooked her.

"I thought it was you," she explained. "I had just turned out my light, my back was to the closed bedroom door. I thought I heard you come into the room and sit down on the bed." She felt the bed sag and move slightly, as if my weight were on the other side. "Well?" Marsha had asked in the dark. "What do you want, Kim?" Upon getting no response, she turned over and saw that no one was there. That was when she had screamed.

I instantly sent my feelers out to every corner of the house to try to identify any other presences among us. What I picked up was that Sally was here. But how? Why was I sensing her as a spirit? She could drive over from eastern Washington anytime she wanted—why would she visit in an out-of-body state? Not wanting to further frighten Marsha, who was still bug-eyed with alarm, I reassured her that probably she had had a dream as she was falling asleep. (It was the same explanation I'd given myself when I'd seen demons.) She went back to bed, leaving her door open—just in case.

The next morning, as we were getting ready for work, Marsha came into my bedroom. There was something she wanted to show me on the bathroom mirror. I followed her into the bathroom, where we both stared in silence at what appeared to be words, etched faintly in strange handwriting on the surface of the mirror. Though vowels followed consonants in a pronounceable pattern, the words were not in any language that either of us recognized. Again, I invented a plausible story. The inscription had probably always been there, I said; we'd just never noticed it before. Again, she accepted my explanation because I think she wanted to. But I knew better.

That night, lying in my own bed after turning out the light, I heard what sounded like a knock on the door. It couldn't be Marsha—she never knocked. In the dim light, I saw the antique doorknob turn and the door slowly swung open about two feet. No one was there that I could see, but I felt Sally's presence—I was absolutely certain of it. My bed sagged, as if from a phantom weight, and the sheets and covers on the left side moved slightly. This was definitely no dream—my eyes were open. Wide open.

Something was wrong. Sally wasn't supposed to be here. I had the strong sense that somehow Sally was no longer among the living, and was stuck in a sort of limbo. She was "punching through" from her reality to ours, to this house she loved so much. She couldn't let go. This was going to cause problems for all of us if she kept hanging around. Someone needed to set her straight, and I figured that someone was me.

"Sally," I said out loud, feeling idiotic for conversing with a ghost, "this is freaking me out and it's freaking Marsha out. I know this is you, Sally, and I know that you love this house, but you need to go. God is waiting for you. You have to trust that I will always care for your beautiful house. Sally, if you go to the wonderful Light of God that's waiting for you, I promise you I'll make sure that in my lifetime, every owner of this house will care for it with the same kind of love you gave it. You know how much I love this house, too. I promise you that its walls will only know love, but you need to let go. You need to go to the Light."

Had I said the right things? I could detect no response from Sally. I lay back on the bed again, tried to relax, and simply began to chew the fat with her. I talked about all the improvements I'd made on the house—how I'd cleaned it up, insulated, painted, put in gardens, replaced the furnace. I chatted as if she were a girlfriend who'd dropped by for a cup of tea—it felt that comfortable. Eventually, I drifted off to sleep.

AFTER THE LIGHT

Sally never visited us again, but we soon heard news of her. A neighbor told us Sally had been involved in a collision with a drunken driver near the little town of Twisp, east of the Cascade Mountains. At the time her ghost came calling on us, Sally had been dead for several weeks.

By the autumn of 1985, I had been interviewed for thirty newspaper and magazine articles, radio shows, and television programs on the subject of near-death experiences. I had also conducted more than fifty presentations and workshops on the subject, as well as on death and dying. Before each one, I silently prayed that whatever I said would be in accordance with God's wishes. Though I had an outline, my style was to speak extemporaneously, and I felt strongly that I did not do it alone—I had the assistance of a higher power. The appearances filled me with energy, both from my own enthusiasm and love for the subject, and the energy I felt from the audience.

Yet in all this time, I deliberately never mentioned that I had had a near-death experience. I still believed that such an admission would undermine the professional reputation I had worked so hard to build. My fear was that audiences would, at the very least, perceive me as biased toward mystical or spiritual interpretations of near-death events. At the worst, they would write me off as a flake. My message—that death holds nothing to fear, that the realization of that fact enables us all to live our lives more fully—would be lost.

In October 1985, I conducted a presentation on the near-death experience to an organization of oncology social workers. During the question-and-answer period that followed, a forest of hands waved in the air. As usual, there were more questions than I had time to answer—questions of the type I'd heard before.

People wanted to know if it was possible to have a scary near-death experience. What about suicide attempters—what happens to them? What about pets?

Eventually, there was time for only one more question. A hand shot up from the back row and a woman's voice carried clearly all the way across the room. "I'd like to know if you have ever had a near-death experience," she said.

Standing at the podium, I froze. This was the question I'd been dreading and avoiding for fifteen years, and now it was in front of me and could not be ignored. Mentally, I paced furiously around the stage, wringing my hands and bemoaning my predicament. *What'll I do?* I asked myself. *I can't tell a lie, but how can I reveal the truth? Oh, dear, oh dear. What will I do?*

The audience saw only a blank expression on my face as the question hung in the air, unanswered. People began to exchange glances with one another. I had to say something, but I was struck dumb with fear. Then into my head popped the Chinese symbol for crisis, which an Asian patient of mine had given me on a card. The symbol combines two characters—one for danger, the other for opportunity. That was it. Answering the question truthfully might be dangerous, but it also posed an opportunity for me. I might as well see where that opportunity led, and let the chips fall where they may. No matter what, I could never deny my own near-death experience.

Leaning forward into the microphone, in a voice barely above a whisper, I broke the uneasy silence. "Yes," I told the audience. "Yes, I have." I told them I had never admitted my near-death experience in public because no one had ever asked me the Big Question. "Of course, it took a crowd of social workers to draw this information out of me," I added with a wan smile.

Now I faced a whole new set of questions, which I'd never answered in public before. My listeners were full of curiosity about what had happened to me. What was my near-death experience like? How had it changed me? We stayed well after the allotted time for the presentation so I could respond to their seemingly boundless hunger for firsthand information.

This became a defining moment in my career, because I learned that I had been wrong. Being honest about my experience didn't hurt my credibility. If anything, it seemed to enhance it. From then on, I didn't have to limit myself to a dispassionate recitation of the various elements of a near-death experience and the statistics on its incidence, livened up with other people's stories. I didn't have to pretend to be emotionally detached from discussion of the phenomenon that had been the single most important force for change in my life. I was free to speak from the heart, as well as from my social worker's notebook.

Maybe it was a sign of the times. In the mid-1980s, I noticed a sea change in the attitude of total strangers about my work. In the past, if I met someone at a party who asked me what I did, I knew exactly how they would react to my answer. Their eyes would glaze over or begin darting around the room in search of a more suitable conversation partner. It was a bit much that both Don and I were professionals in fields where death was a constant everyday occurrence. "People are dying to see us," was Don's standard quip.

Now people reacted differently when I told them I was in charge of social services for cancer patients and their families and was deeply involved in educating people about death, dying, and the near-death experience. They no longer backpedaled away. They still didn't want to talk about dying, per se. But the possibility of an afterlife, which seemed to be confirmed in near-death experiences, caused them to question me further. Are our souls eternal? they wanted to know. Will they endure after our bodies have died? How will we pass from this world to the next? In fairly short order, I had gone from being a pariah at a party to someone who was not only worth talking to, but seeking out.

On the home front, I was also entering a new phase in my relationship with Don. After arriving in Leawood for Christmas with my family, Don called to say that he was going to hop a plane and join us. Home with the whole family for the holidays? This sounded serious and, indeed, Don was a man with a mission.

There was joy in Mudville the night when Don was to arrive, except that he didn't. He didn't arrive the night he was scheduled, nor the next night, nor the next night, nor even the fourth night thereafter. The national news day after day was of the huge bank of fog that was socking in the entire Pacific Northwest. This weather pattern, not uncommon in winter, was making history by its density and duration. There was no air travel out of Seattle.

After five days, Don called to say that he was giving up, not his attempts, but his methods. Abandoning hope of catching a flight out of Sea-Tac Airport, he boarded the next bus out of town, which was headed for Spokane. Perhaps he could fly from there. The long bus ride across state already was going to be made longer by the treacherousness of driving over fog and snowbound mountains. But the trip loomed eternal as Don viewed the only two available seats—one next to a seven-year-old girl who had a week's worth of dot-to-dot puzzles on her lap, and the other one next to a morbidly obese man who had parked his wad of chewed gum on his forehead while he guzzled a beer. Don played dot-to-dot for eleven hours.

Late at night, when the bus arrived in Spokane, Don was greeted by more fog. He prayed that he would reach me by Christmas, and I prayed his prayers would be answered.

A few hours later, a shot of early-morning sunlight hit the airfield. Don was on the one plane sitting in the sun that had a chance to get out. The plane took off, and then, mystically, the airport was again enshrouded in a thick fog that kept it closed for the next day and half. But Don's travails were not over. The flight landed in Denver, where he found himself snowed in at Stapleton International Airport. Finally, on Christmas Eve, he showed up at the homestead—cash poor, bewhiskered, unshowered, and ready to kiss the cold Kansas ground.

The next morning in the midst of the melee as my family tore into their gifts, I opened a small jewelry box that contained a necklace in the shape of half of a heart with a small diamond upon it. Captivated, I looked at Don. "If you marry me," he said, "I'll give you a bigger diamond and the rest of my heart." I thought it was a real good deal.

Don was good to his word on both counts. On Valentine's Day evening, he escorted me to a classy Pike Place Market restaurant where a gaggle of employees showed us to a table banked with masses of floral arrangements from Don. As we took our seats amid the flora, Don looked at me lovingly and seriously. So did the staff. They, along with a ring of diners surrounding our table, watched as Don reached into his inside coat pocket and pulled out a small ring box. With a smile of shy anticipation, he slid it across the table in my direction. Staring back adoringly at him, I picked up the box and opened it. It was empty. Laughing, Don reached into another part of his jacket and pulled out a small, white teddy bear. The teddy bear was holding a red satin heart and pinned to the heart was a thin gold band bearing a large round diamond surrounded by three marquise-shaped diamonds. The effect was like a flower caught in a gust of wind. While I stared in shock at the splendor of the ring, the diners and waiters burst into applause. We were officially engaged.

Now it was full steam ahead to the altar, which we found in a beautiful church above the West Seattle ferry dock. The interior was an enormous echo of Noah's Ark in natural wood tones that framed a story-and-a-half glass wall overlooking a rhododendron garden. I could have worn a potato sack and still looked good in front of that window.

On the afternoon of July 13, 1986, the bridal dressing room was fanned by yards and yards of watermelon-red moiré taffeta as the three bridesmaids donned their gowns. Their dresses were full length, elegant, strapless—almost daring. In contrast, I was covered from head to toe. In lieu of a potato sack, I wore a floor-length white organza lace-and-pearl gown. Mutton sleeves and a six-foot train were set off by my pearl crown and fingertip tulle veil. Powder and hair spray drifted outside to the parking lot, where the menfolk gathered around a contraband cooler of Rainier Beer.

The church overflowed with baskets of red, pink, and white flowers. Flowers hung from altars, candelabras, windows, pillars, and pews. Against the towering glass altar wall the church seemed to be a part of an elaborate outdoor garden, laced like floral needlepoint with red silk ribbon.

Ushers and groomsmen dressed in black tuxes with watermelon-red satin bow ties and cummerbunds seated the arriving guests. Friends and family from every corner of the country came to see for sure that we were *really* going to finally marry. My mom looked triumphant. It had taken God twenty years to answer her prayers for my marriage, and now it was becoming a reality. I fully expected her to jump up and high-five my dad's upraised hand when the ceremony was over.

As the organ music switched to the "Trumpet Voluntary," Don, dressed like his groomsmen but wearing a white tuxedo jacket instead of black, slapped yet one more brace of aftershave on his face and then led the men and his eleven-year-old son, Andy, to the front of the assemblage.

My sister Kristy, the maid of honor, followed the other bridesmaids down the sixty-foot aisle, bringing dignity and serenity with her Grace Kelly bearing—belying her constant fear that her chest would not hold up the top of her gown.

Don's eight-year-old daughter, Jennifer, dressed like a miniature bride, froze just before her entrance as the flower girl. We confabbed under my veil as I bent over her to ascertain the source of her distress. She was afraid she was going to botch evenly distributing the flower petals that she held in a wicker basket. She took my advice to forget about petaling and concentrate on pedaling. Off she ran, sprinting to her brother, who awaited her in his little black tux.

Then it was "Here Comes the Bride," both on the organ and on the arm of my dad. A blitzkrieg of flashes announced my last few moments as a single woman. Dad teared up as he lifted my veil to kiss me when we reached Don at the end of the bridal path. Don in turn kissed Dad on the forehead and escorted me to the altar.

My uncle, the Reverend Dean Lueking, performed the ceremony. Uncle Dean spoke with such eloquence and spiritual authority that several guests, unaware he pastored at Grace Lutheran Church in Chicago, returned to the wedding church the following Sunday to hear his sermon. Brother Paul sang songs, including a duet with Kristy that got the sacred attention of every angel in the place. Impending marriage had not affected my angel vision, though I was not going to let even angels distract me from this service. Dean reminded us of angels, however, and those in their heavenly company—Don's dad, Eugene Sharp, and my grandmother, Tyra Lueking, who was Dean's mom.

The tidal movements of Don's and my life finally came together when Uncle Dean asked us to promise aloud to take each other from that day forward. A cloud of monarch butterflies of such volume and height that it momentarily absorbed our attention suddenly took flight on the other side of the glass wall. Then we said, "I do," exchanged rings, and became husband and wife to thundering cheers and applause of the hundreds of witnesses to our love.

Marriage was a breeze compared to my new job. Professionally, I was beginning to feel as if I had jumped from the frying pan into the fire. The "Hutch" was a huge research institution, sprawling over several blocks, and its various fiefdoms were well established long before I arrived on the scene. In the organizational scheme of things, the new department of social work was to be perpetually understaffed, underfunded, and overworked.

One of my first battles was over the lack of walls to create private counseling areas within the large open room which comprised the department's new quarters. Instead, we were given cheesy corkboard room dividers, less than five feet tall. Every patient, family member, and marrow donor coming to the Hutch was reeling from shock, fear, and despair, and it was the social workers to whom they poured out their hearts. Separated only by a few small dividers, these distraught people had no privacy; their every word could be heard all over the room. Finally, we got walls—not real ones, but mattress-size, sound-absorbing, temporary panels that we hereafter referred to as the Kotex pads. The makeshift solution was an inauspicious omen.

The need for counseling services was enormous. A bone marrow transplant required a hundred days of hospitalization and follow-up care, a wrenching experience for patients and their families. Every transplant was a gamble; the only sure thing was that the patient would die without it. Even for donors, the procedure was arduous, draining. There were a huge number of outpatients, many of whom needed services of one kind or another.

My days were spent rushing from meeting to meeting, juggling resources, maneuvering through the institutional minefields. Even on my worst days at Harborview, I still felt confident of my capabilities. At the Hutch, I seemed always to be struggling toward impossible goals—a day late and a dollar short.

When Pacific Northwest Magazine named me as one of the most influential people in the Northwest under the age of forty, my sagging self-esteem got a much-needed boost. It also brought widespread media attention to me and my position at the Hutch. Unfortunately, it was not the sort of publicity my employers wanted. The recognition was due to my contributions to the field of death and dying—both of which the Hutch was loath to acknowledge. Death was the enemy. The world-renowned Fred Hutchinson Cancer Research Center stood for defeating cancer and defeating death, not accepting it. From the chilly response that my temporary celebrity generated at work, I knew that my days there were numbered.

I was numbering other days as well—those of my menstrual cycle. I wanted a baby desperately. Don had had a vasectomy seven years earlier, and soon after our marriage, underwent the outrageously expensive microsurgery that might—or might not—restore his fertility. Because of the length of time since the original procedure, and other complications, the doctors gave us little encouragement that the surgery would be successful. A few months later, Don's sperm count was still zero. With more faith than hope, we ignored the naysayers and kept trying to have a baby.

One morning in September 1987, our faith was rewarded. After Don left for work, I opened the take-home pregnancy test kit I had secretly purchased the day before and spread out the contents in the bathroom. I felt like a mad scientist preparing a clandestine experiment. I poured a sample of my urine into a vial, dropped in a little stick, and walked away, trying to distract myself for the next five minutes by dressing for work. After the prescribed time had elapsed, I nervously went into the bathroom and beheld the stick. It had turned blue—undeniably, blessedly, blue. That meant I was pregnant. I was so astonished my legs gave out and I sank down on the toilet seat, staring in disbelief at the magical blue stick. A baby, a baby, we were going to have a baby.

Hurriedly, I finished dressing and left for work. I couldn't wait to call Don and tell him. However, as soon as I got to the office, I was called to a meeting with my supervisor. There I received the second shocking news of the day: I was fired. My phone call to Don didn't go quite as I had expected.

"Honey, hi," I said in a quavery voice when Don answered the phone at his Medic One office.

"Hi," said Don with his usual good cheer. "What's up?"

"I'm pregnant. And I'm fired," I blurted, sobbing into the receiver.

There was a long pause. Then I heard the distinct sound of my husband throwing up.

I soon became so fascinated and absorbed with pregnancy that I got over the shock of losing my job. Though our growing family was now dependent on one income, I was ridiculously happy. I was thirty-nine years old and never had felt better, more alive, or more important. This was an incredible, miraculous gift I'd received, a gift of life that only I could bring to fruition.

I was surrounded by angel babies—or so said my old friend Margaret Burrell, who taught infant massage to nurses in Hawaii. Margaret lived in Honolulu, and we caught up with each other once a year in a long, chatty phone call at Christmas. Margaret was famous for her uncannily accurate visions, which came to her in dreams. When Margaret called that Christmas, she told me about one of her dreams. She and I were together in an ethereal place, and the air was thick with angel babies. I was lying on a gurney with intravenous tubes in both arms, which were connected to bottles. The angel babies had brought the bottles, which were full of material that would give me the physical and spiritual strength to bear one of the babies. Margaret had the dream in August, the month I conceived. She had no idea I was pregnant until she called me.

As for myself, I could no longer see angels. I discovered this shortly before Christmas when I attended a piano concert to benefit Seattle IANDS. The music was lovely and there were angels everywhere—I was quite used to seeing them on such occasions. Suddenly, without any sign that it was happening, I felt the spirit of the baby enter my body. "The baby's here," I gasped to Betty Preston, my coleader of the IANDS group. I had the certain knowledge that its spirit was within me, but not yet confined to me; it could still come and go. At the same time, the angels vanished. One moment I could see them, the next moment I couldn't. I sensed that they were still there, but that the presence of the baby's spirit somehow blocked them from my vision.

My wonderful obstetrician, Judith Jacobsen, determined my due date to be May 19, 1988—four days before my fortieth birthday. I was determined that I was going to be a mom while still in my thirties. Too bad I couldn't speed the process a little more. As the months went by, my enchantment with pregnancy declined in direct proportion to my increasing discomfort. At the rate I was gaining weight, I feared my formerly slender, five-foot, five-inch frame would resemble a blimp by the time I gave birth. It did.

By the beginning of May I felt like Dolly Parton lugging a watermelon. I had a forty-one-inch waist, wore an industrial-strength 36E bra, and was so off balance that I walked slightly sideways, like a swollen crab. No one expected me to make it to the due date—least of all, me. The nursery was ready, fully stocked with baby T-shirts, footie pajamas, and receiving blankets. Dr. Judi and the rest of my birthing team were ready. My parents flew in from Kansas, stocked the refrigerator, cleaned the house, and were now tapping their feet—they were ready. Don and I had taken six weeks of childbirth classes and we were definitely ready. But the baby wasn't.

My fortieth birthday came and went—still, no baby. I had talked about renting a cruise ship, having a big party, and going dancing under the stars. Instead, my blood pressure soared and Dr. Judi ordered me off my feet. What really depressed me was that my medical chart would now list me as an "aged primigravida," or advanced maternal age, meaning a woman whose first baby was born after the age of forty. I took to my bed in a snit.

Finally, on June 1, the doctor scheduled me for induced labor the next morning. That evening I went into labor, hard and fast. The contractions were so close together that Don called Medic One for transportation to the hospital. Don had helped deliver three babies but he had no intention of delivering his own. Not wanting to alarm the neighborhood, he identified himself to the dispatcher—Don was a Medic One supervisor—and asked that the ambulance be sent "quietly." When the boss calls 911 and asks for an ambulance vehicle to come quietly, nobody pays attention. Within minutes, a fleet of emergency vehicles converged on our front lawn—lights flashing, sirens wailing. The neighbors flocked outside and learned the surprising news that I was in labor. They had thought my pregnancy was permanent.

I had carefully packed a bag with playing cards, massage oil, portable tape player, relaxing audiotapes, and a "focal point" to concentrate on during labor: a tiny newborn T-shirt. It was supposed to encourage me to get through labor and delivery naturally, without drugs, breathing through the pain the way the childbirth instructor had taught. I never did find that darn bag, and by the time I got to the hospital, I deeply regretted I hadn't paid more attention in those birthing classes. I had daydreamed a lot because I figured that if anyone would have an out-of-body experience during labor, it would be yours truly. I would just check out of my body during the hard part. Piece of cake.

The trouble was, I stayed completely in my body. The pain was unbearable and unrelieved. Within a couple of hours, I was fully dilated to ten centimeters and putting on quite a show. My head was ready to start spinning in circles like Linda Blair's in *The Exorcist. Forget natural childbirth,* I thought. In a brief pause between contractions, I grabbed the stiff white collar of the nurse who hovered next to my bed and yanked her down close to my grimacing face. Between clenched teeth I hissed, "Get me the anesthesiologist, and I will name this baby after him."

I pushed her toward the door, where she reappeared moments later with the anesthesiologist. "Oh, no," I exclaimed when I read his ID tag. His name? Dr. Highness. Not even *I* would refer to my baby as Your Highness, no matter how royally we planned to treat it.

I was given an epidural, which quickly numbed me from the waist down. It was a relief to be out of pain, but the fetal monitor indicated the baby's heartbeat had dangerously slowed. They were prepping me for a C-section when the obstetrician on duty walked in. "Vaht do we have here?" she asked in an authoritative voice with a thick Eastern European accent. *I* looked up to see an imposing female figure, sort of a cross between Nurse Ratched and a Prussian commander. Where, oh, where was my sweet Dr. Judi?

Even the baby seemed to snap to attention, for its heartbeat

197
▼

returned to normal. The plans for a C-section were scrapped. Upon examining me, however, the doctor discovered another problem. "Vell, vell," she announced. "It seems that the baby is backvurds. Vee vill take care of this right now." With that, she picked up a scalpel, performed a quick episiotomy to enlarge the birth canal, and *reached inside* to turn the baby around. It felt as if she were using both hands and both arms, too. I was sure they never talked about this in childbirth class.

With the baby reoriented in the right direction, the doctor commanded me to *push*. Obediently, I pushed—for two and a half hours. It felt like I pushed us to San Francisco and back. Now I understood the true meaning of "labor." Finally, at 1:26 A.M. on June 2, 1988, the baby was born. "It's a girl!" someone said. She weighed a hefty eight pounds, three ounces, had teal-blue eyes, and cheeks so fat that I immediately understood why it had taken so long to push her out. Her most distinctive feature was her hair—reddish blond, long, and gummed straight up with the waxy substance that coated her strong body. Her brother, Andy, remarked that she looked just like Don King, the electric-haired boxing promoter.

We named her Rebecca Clark Sharp. She was flesh of my flesh, a combination of our genes and our spiritual gifts, a living miracle, the promise of the future, our very own angel baby.

CHAPTER THIRTEEN

THE "C" WORD

▼

TWO DAYS AFTER giving birth to Rebecca, I was ready to leave the hospital except for a nagging little problem: I couldn't urinate. After much testing and examining, it was determined that Rebecca's birth had been even more violent than I thought. My bladder had been pushed up under my rib cage. It was collecting urine, but refused to release it. A catheter was put in place and I promptly got a bladder infection.

All this was occurring at the same time that I was falling off a hormonal cliff into a black pit of depression. I felt like I was spinning helplessly down a drain, unable to stop the downward spiral. Was this the much-touted joy of motherhood? How would I survive?

I prayed.

It was late at night. Don, who had spent every night in the hospital room with me, was asleep. Rebecca was in the nursery. All was quiet when I had my heart-to-heart with God. I asked for the strength to achieve a better frame of mind, more emotional stability, and some modicum of happiness, which seemed to be slipping away during what I thought was going to be the best time of my life.

God came through for me. In the morning, I was transferred

to a new room, a big corner room with lots of light. It was soon filled with well-wishers, flowers, and balloons—just the boost I needed. Doctor Judi assured me that these feelings I was having were normal, and she gave me some literature on postpartum depression. Just reading about it made me feel better. It's funny how knowing that something is normal can be such a relief. It reminded me of my mission to normalize the near-death experience. To think that someday doctors could give their patients pamphlets that read, "What happened to you is normal. It's called a near-death experience. This is what you can expect as a result. . . . "

A week later, I went home with the catheter still in place and a urine bag strapped to my left thigh like a holster, trailing a charming tube from my urethra. I had strict instructions not to lift Rebecca. June was a miserable month, made gloomy by leaden skies and the sort of cold, wet weather Seattle is famous for when it's summer everywhere else. Within a day, I was bedridden with a fever, unable to care for Rebecca or do all the little things that new mothers do for their babies. Except for breastfeeding, Don stoically carried the whole load. The combination of postpartum depression, pain, illness, bad weather, and a fussy baby had me immobilized with self-pity.

Don was outside and I was trying to take a nap when I heard Rebecca screaming from her crib. Our bedroom was on the far side of the house from the nursery but I covered the distance as if I had wings. I looked into her crib and saw that she was vomiting. Instinctively, I reached down and picked her up. The pain in my insides was searing, but I could not drop Rebecca. Carrying her in one arm and using the other to support myself along the walls, I got us both back to my bedroom.

I flopped down hard on the bed. The catheter ripped out, bringing with it a flood of blood and urine. Rebecca then contributed her vomit to this mess. She looked at me, I looked at her, and we both burst into tears. We had ourselves one heck of a cry. It bonded us completely. I felt there was a little spirit in that baby who perfectly understood how awful things were, and was willing to share the moment with me anyway. I realized how self-absorbed I'd been, thinking I had so much to deal with—without even noticing the monumental adjustments Rebecca was having to make to this strange new world. It humbled me.

Again, I turned to prayer—this time, on a large scale. My mother, my brother, my sister, and a number of friends belonged to prayer circles around the country. The word went out to pray that my health would return, that the hateful catheter would be removed, and that I would assume what had become the most important task in my life, taking care of this little girl. The prayers were answered. In a few days, my bladder function returned to normal and the catheter was removed.

Rebecca was only a few weeks old when I was asked to appear in a pilot for a new television series on paranormal events to be hosted by William Shatner. They were calling it *The Enigma File.* The producers would pay my expenses to come to Los Angeles for the taping of a segment on near-death experiences; they would even provide child care if I brought Rebecca. I said yes, instantly.

Nothing ever came of the television pilot, but the trip was a nice two-day getaway, memorable for the manner in which Rebecca and I arrived and departed Los Angeles. We were met at the airport by a black limousine—almost as common as taxicabs in L.A.—and a friendly driver. On the way to our hotel, the driver filled me in on the passing sights, and politely asked me what I was doing in town. I told him about the show.

"Hey—my dad's had a near-death experience," he said. I told

him I'd like to hear about it. He asked when I was leaving, I told him my schedule, and he said, "I'll pass this along to my dad. He might want to tell you his story himself."

Sure enough, when Rebecca and I left the television studio the next day for the airport, the father was waiting to take us. He was a dignified, handsome, silver-haired gent—the owner of the limousine company and the epitome of a Hollywood chauffeur. He showed us to a silver-and-white limo as long and sleek as the Concorde. Now *this* was a limousine. The interior was like a luxuriously appointed hotel on wheels—bouquets of fresh flowers, a crystal decanter and glasses, fruit drinks and bottled waters for a nursing mother, an elegantly displayed box of diaper wipes for Rebecca. The man had thought of everything.

Zipping along the freeways, he told me about his near-death experience. Like every near-death experiencer, he was glad to find someone who not only listened to him but believed him. He was so grateful that when we arrived at the airport, he told me to wait in the limo while he took my baggage and checked me in. That must be how the stars do it—you never see them standing in line with crying babies. I was content to stay inside this incredible vehicle for hours—days, in fact.

Meanwhile, passersby began to congregate outside on the sidewalk. Unable to see beyond the limo's darkened windows, they were waiting to see who the bigshot celebrity was. More and more people joined the crowd, some of them with cameras. Obviously tourists. I adjusted my absorbent breast pads and fluffed my hair. With erect military bearing, our chauffeur flung open the door and stepped aside. Carrying Rebecca in my arms, I emerged to the scattered flash of camera bulbs and the murmur of the crowd. Then silence. Someone could stand it no longer. "Who are *you?*" she asked.

"Teri Garr," I replied, walking briskly into the airport.

"Gee," I heard a voice drifting behind me. "I didn't know she had a baby."

For the first two years of Rebecca's life, I willingly traded my attaché case for a diaper bag and made my family my first priority. Yet I still maintained my academic position as a clinical assistant professor by continuing to publish articles and lecture from time to time at the University of Washington School of Medicine and other area colleges. Since I wasn't restricted by a regular job, I could increase the number of presentations I made in other parts of the country. By Rebecca's second birthday, she had been in sixteen states and was a seasoned traveler.

I also fell in with a group of women who had daughters Rebecca's age. We had met when our babies were a year old and became inseparable friends. We all had satisfying, demanding careers and were now on the mommy track full time. We called ourselves the Hens. Though we each had very different personalities, we bonded to each other like glue. Those friendships would become, literally, my lifeline.

In August 1990, I flew to Washington, D.C., to attend the first International Conference on Near-Death Studies at Georgetown University. I had recently weaned Rebecca and this was my first big trip without her. The conference, sponsored by IANDS, drew more than three hundred attendees and was a huge success. But there was an undertone of sadness. All of us IANDS old-timers missed the presence of sociologist Chuck Flynn, one of the IANDS board members who had died by his own hand several years earlier. He was a sweet, huggy-bear kind of guy; it was a shame he died too soon to witness the international growth of IANDS. "Gee, I wish Chuck could see this," said board member Barbara Harris as her eyes swept the crowded banquet room on the final evening of the conference. "He would be so amazed."

Later on, as I sat listening to one of the speakers, it was my turn to be amazed. I felt Chuck's spirit enter my body. As had happened with George, I felt as if I were sharing space within my flesh. I had full consciousness and awareness, but someone else was in charge. I also felt as if I weighed a ton. Chuck was a big man—at least six-feet, four-inches tall and heavyset; he would have dwarfed me even at my maximum pregnancy weight. My feet, which had been resting on the chair in front of me, felt too heavy to move.

Chuck wanted something, I knew that, but I wasn't sure what. As the banquet ended and people started leaving, I could feel his excitement as people he knew passed by. I felt this wasn't the first time Chuck had been in the presence of his friends since his death, but it was the first time so many of them were together at the same time. Maybe he just wanted to be part of the party.

The room was clearing out, and there I continued to sit, weighted down by Chuck. When the staff began folding up the tables and chairs, I realized it was time to make a move. "Chuck, we've got to get up," I said. It worked. "We" got up and walked clumsily out of the room into an adjacent foyer. Obviously, we were physically not very well matched, but I felt totally plugged into Chuck's consciousness. This went both ways; I was also completely exposed to him. I knew he was on a mission, and I decided to trust him in whatever it was. He could borrow my body to accomplish it.

Chuck's agenda became clear as soon as we approached Raymond Moody. What Chuck wanted was for Raymond, Kenneth Ring, and Bruce Greyson—three preeminent researchers and writers in the field of near-death studies, whom we both knew through their association with IANDS—to get together, chew the fat, and raise a glass in memory of Chuck Flynn. It was just that simple. I said something to Raymond—or rather, Chuck did—and he went off to find Ken and Bruce. The last I saw of them, they said they were going up to Ken's room to tell Chuck Flynn stories. Chuck went with them, leaving me in peace and feeling hundreds of pounds lighter.

In December 1990, I had a mammogram, my second. The first had been a few months after Rebecca's birth. Dr. Judi called to let me know that something had shown up on the latest mammogram, and she was sending it to radiology for a closer look. The spot was very small, on the outer quadrant of my left breast, almost off the X ray. She reassured me it was probably a little cyst or something benign. Dr. Judi had just given me my annual physical and breast exam, and I was clean as a whistle, so there was probably nothing to worry about. Probably.

Even after the radiologist recommended a biopsy, Don and I were optimistic. We saw the surgeon Dr. Judi had recommended late in the day on New Year's Eve. From my Harborview days, I remembered him as an artist with the scalpel. As he examined me, he was unable to feel any lumps in the area where the mammogram showed a spot. That was a good sign, he said. He would take out the suspicious tissue in a simple surgical procedure called a lumpectomy that would be done on an outpatient basis in the same building as his office. No muss, no fuss. I'd be able to go dancing that very night, he promised.

No one ever mentioned cancer.

A week and a half later, Don and I returned for the lumpectomy and biopsy. A nurse showed me to a "proce-e-e-e-dure" room. She stretched out the pronunciation just that way, so that the word had an ominous ring to it. This was my introduction to perhaps the single most dreaded word in cancer treatment circles:

procedure. I was about to learn firsthand that *procedure* was usually a euphemism for something unpleasant or painful or both.

A technician arranged my breast in the giant tortilla press of the mammogram machine, and a radiologist slid an extremely long, slender needle into my breast until it touched the suspicious spot shown on the X ray. Then he told me I could go back in the waiting room where I would be called for surgery. I was dumbfounded. The needle still protruded from my chest, along with several inches of wire. What if I bumped into something and the needle was jammed in farther, maybe into my lung? Gingerly draping the hospital gown around me, I self-consciously walked back into a waiting room filled with people, all fully clothed. Another introduction—this time, to the thoughtless indignities to which patients of every stripe are subjected.

After the surgery, I awoke in a recovery room and definitely did not feel like going dancing. My left side bulged with bandages and white tape under my hospital gown. The surgeon was in great spirits. He'd found the lump and sent it to pathology for biopsy. "It didn't look like a cyst," he said, "but whatever it was, it looked benign. Don't worry. I'll see you in a few days for follow-up. Make an appointment with the nurse on your way out."

At ten that night, he called me with unexpected news. The initial pathology report indicated the growth was malignant after all. However, it was "in situ"—contained all in one place, like a nut within a shell. This was good, and the surgeon still sounded upbeat. "It's outta there, Kim. It's gone. Get a good night's sleep. Don't worry."

He called again the next morning, this time with the full pathology report. The tumor was not contained; it had spirals, like a comet with spinning tails. The spirals were still in my body. In fact, the projected path of tumor growth was the tissue around the lymph glands under my left arm. "We're going to have to schedule you for more extensive surgery," he said. "I want to do this as soon as possible."

Tumor. Malignancy. The words spun in my head. I felt dizzy. But the awful word, the "c" word—*cancer*—had not been spoken.

Thousands of miles away in Hawaii, Margaret Burrell made a drawing of me with pen and ink. She drew me the way she had seen me in a vision: head, neck, shoulders, arms, bare breasts. On the far side of my left breast she drew a small dark circle with spiraling tentacles and labeled it "hot spot." Her pen would not draw anything below my rib cage. She thought that was odd, and put the drawing away.

I spent the weekend calling family and close friends. I didn't beat around the bush, or use words like tumor or malignancy. I said, "I have breast cancer." In the days that followed, I was businesslike, organized. In addition to preparing myself and our household for major surgery and convalescence, I also arranged all the major speakers at a conference I was chairing in August on the near-death experience. I wasn't going to let this cancer thing dominate my life, or even upset my schedule. I had it all together. Until I noticed I was doing things like putting a cup of coffee in the toaster oven and turning the dial to "dark." Underneath it all, I was incredibly distracted and worried.

Every time I talked with the surgeon, the news got worse. Now he told me that I had an unusual malignancy for someone my age—what he called an "old lady's tumor," close to the chest wall. In older women, the malignancy is usually manageable because cell growth is slower. But in my relatively young body it was growing very rapidly. He didn't know what to make of it.

I insisted on a second opinion. I wanted to talk to an oncologist—a cancer specialist—and asked him for a referral. I couldn't help but be reminded of an old joke, often told at Fred Hutchinson. It goes like this: An oncologist and a surgeon go duck hunting. They wait for the birds in two separate blinds. The oncologist sees a flock taking off. He thinks, "Hmmm. They look like ducks, they sound like ducks—they must be ducks." He raises his shotgun. *Bam, bam, bam.* The surgeon, meanwhile, just goes *bam, bam, bam.* "Hey," he calls out to his friend. "Were those ducks?"

The oncologist the surgeon referred me to was Henry Kaplan. I knew all about Dr. Kaplan, who was with the Tumor Institute of Swedish Hospital and Medical Center. He'd had several patients at the Hutch who underwent bone marrow transplants. His reputation as a cancer doctor was impeccable: obsessively committed, unrelentingly honest, and very, very knowledgeable. He agreed to see Don and me that same evening.

The outcome of our meeting was so heartening that after we got home I wrote in my journal, "The sunny rays of hope pierced the darkness today in the form of Dr. Henry Kaplan. We went in seeking a second opinion and two hours later had found 'my doctor.' Happily, he will follow me through the valley of the shadow of cancer and out again. I feel good and it feels so good to feel good. The diagnosis doesn't sound so grim. He was so informative and clear and sincere and huggable that it gave me courage and spunk. He was also the first doctor to say the word *cancer*."

My surgery was set for January 23. In the meantime, I talked on the phone to Chris Horner, a neighbor my age whose kids played with my kids. We sort of knew about each other, but we'd never met before. Now we found out we had both been diagnosed with breast cancer on the same day; we both had Dr. Kaplan as an oncologist; and we were both scheduled for surgery on the same day at the same hospital. As we marveled at this coincidence, Chris told me that she had been inspired by a woman she'd seen the week before on a local TV talk show. In front of a live audience, the woman had spoken honestly about the spiritual aspect of dying and near-death experiences. Chris had even taken notes; she wanted to share them with me so I could be inspired, too. I didn't need them. The woman on the show was me.

As Chris related to me the very words I had spoken, it was as though I was hearing them for the first time. Only a week ago, I was the authority. I was the one to give advice, provide inspiration. Now I was the patient, and I was hearing these words as almost an entirely different person, a stranger in a strange land—a newly diagnosed cancer patient in need of hope.

I was also in need of laughs. My sense of humor was the one thing—besides prayer and faith—that had seen me through hard times before. For now, I tried to forget how angry I felt about getting cancer, and focus on the humorous aspects of the situation. Strangely, there were some. And when I couldn't find anything funny, I made it up.

Like the outfit I wore for the luncheon the Hens gave for me. I wore a black, strapless, full-length evening gown, black high heels, huge rhinestone earrings, and a black fur coat—in the middle of the day. The surgeon had told me that the only thing I probably wouldn't be able to wear after a partial mastectomy was a strapless top, so I figured it was now or never. The Hens gave me a champagne bottle that they had tastelessly decoupaged with pictures of breasts and funny headlines about boobs, and we partied the afternoon away. I wore my outfit to the grocery store, to my after-school car pool with Andy and Jennifer, to the supper table. I didn't take it off until bedtime.

I rented a TV and VCR for our bedroom and called up the neighborhood video store for a list of all their funny movies. The television rental shop gave me a cancer-patient discount. The owner of the video store, who had herself fought a deadly illness years ago, personally made the list of movies and brought it over, along with a sackful of funny videos that hadn't yet been released to the general public—her own private stash.

On January 22, I entered Swedish Hospital and Medical Center with a chart that identified me as a cancer patient. I was on the other side of the looking glass now—a frightened patient in the territory that I had walked countless times as a calm, reassuring social worker. The entire day was spent being "worked up" for surgery with a multitude of "procedures," including a bone scan. I was poked and probed for hours. They saved the blood tests for last. A technician tied a rubber tube around my arm, cinched it tight, and began drawing one vial of dark red blood after another.

When he was almost done, I asked if he would take one more test. He looked surprised, and said no one had ever asked him to take more blood before. He asked what sort of test I wanted.

"I believe I'm pregnant," I said.

His face went pale as he rolled backward on his stool and hit the counter behind him. "Pregnant? You mean no one has checked that you might be pregnant?"

"No," I said, shaking my head.

"Oh, no, this is bad! This is wrong! This should have been one of the first things done. What've you . . . what've you . . ." His voice trailed away, upset, sputtering. From his reaction I saw I should have mentioned the possibility of pregnancy sooner. But I'd been so blown away by the diagnosis of cancer that I was only dimly aware that I had skipped at least two menstrual periods. They had tested me up one side and down the other; it was surprising they hadn't checked for pregnancy, too. But I was forty-two years old, and I guess no one had thought about it. Another vial of blood was quickly drawn for the pregnancy test.

That night, I went home and slept fitfully. All of my dreams had a sense of doom about them. Surgery was not scheduled until

1:30 P.M., so I spent the morning seeking reassurances from friends and family by phone. They convinced me there was no way I could be pregnant; I needed to put that out of my mind and focus on getting through the surgery and getting well.

This was true. The surgery would remove a sizable portion of my left breast as well as the lymph glands under my left arm. Since we knew cancer cells had already invaded the tissue there, the only question was how many of the lymph nodes were cancerous as well. That would be a good indication of how extensively the cancer may have spread elsewhere. Unavoidably, I would also lose the main nerve and ancillary nerves that extended from my left shoulder to the elbow. Then there would be chemotherapy or radiation or both. It would be a long haul.

Don took me to the hospital at noon and we entered a cubicle in the waiting bay, where patients changed clothes and waited to be taken to the operating room. We had psyched ourselves up for the surgery; we were upbeat, positive, ready to get it over with. I felt like Rocky; I could practically hear the encouraging roar of the crowd as I was being wheeled down the hallway to surgery. Wait a minute—someone really *was* shouting to me. "Stop! Stop!" a voice cried out. "She's pregnant!" My gurney came to a screeching halt.

Back in the waiting bay, the surgeon came in to talk to us. I don't remember what he said. I was thinking about a large framed print that had hung on the wall at the Harborview Burn Center. It was a famous drawing of a long Japanese rowboat filled with people pulling on the oars just as an enormous wave was about to bury them. Someone had drawn an arrow from the endangered rowboat to a caption that read, "You are here." As from a distance, the surgeon's voice reached my ears. I heard the words *therapeutic abortion*. The wave hit and swept me under.

I was about ten or eleven weeks pregnant. My body was

pumping out estrogen that fed the hungry tumor—which explained its astonishing rapid growth. Basically, the surgeon told us I had to choose between my life and that of the fetus. The poisonous regime of cancer treatment would destroy the baby. Without treatment, the cancer would destroy me. The doctor sent us home to think about it. Before we had even left the building, I had made my decision. I was going to have this baby. I didn't care about my own life. All my maternal instincts were saying, "Have the baby. Have the baby. Let the baby live." Don said nothing.

That night, we had an emergency meeting with Dr. Kaplan. I don't know why—maybe because I just didn't want her out of my sight—but we took Rebecca with us. The office was closed, so we had the waiting room to ourselves. Don held me in his arms as I cried, sometimes quietly, sometimes in huge wracking sobs. My eyes were swollen like a prizefighter's from the tears I could not stop. Even when I was exhausted from crying, the tears just kept coming. Rebecca was bewildered by it all.

Dr. Kaplan said I had eight to ten months to live without treatment. He was also afraid the amount of radiation I'd had so far—the bone scan and mammograms—had already impaired the normal growth and development of the fetus. He called a colleague, the head of radiation oncology at the Tumor Institute, who left his dinner table to do the math on how many rads I had received. He concluded that the fetus would be affected, but to what degree was unknown. Kaplan strongly recommended a therapeutic abortion.

Paradoxically, this made me cling to pregnancy more fiercely. It wasn't a fetus, it was a baby, and it had already suffered enough from my horrible disease. I wasn't going to be responsible for ending its life, too. I would rather have my own life end. I wasn't afraid of death. I wanted this baby to be born.

In all this time, Don had not expressed his opinion. Finally, he spoke. He took my hand and said quietly, "Look, Kim, here's my reality. In a few months, I'd be a widower with four children, including one with special needs. I can't do it."

It broke my heart to see his face, so earnest, so filled with pain and love for me. He was right. There was more involved here than just what I wanted. "OK," I sobbed. "OK, but only under certain conditions." I wanted our pastors at Hope Lutheran Church to perform some kind of spiritual baptism for the baby, in absentia. I wanted the baby to have a name. And I wanted Dr. Judi to perform the abortion. This last condition was a big one. Dr. Judi didn't have operating privileges at Swedish, and she was on the staff of a Catholic hospital where she'd signed a contract promising she would not perform abortions. But I had to have her. I knew she would ensure the right emotional and spiritual decorum as she ended my pregnancy—ended what would almost certainly be my last chance to have a baby. I wanted it to be as solemn and sacred an occasion as possible.

As Don drive our car out of the hospital parking garage into the dark street, we heard Rebecca's little voice from her car seat behind us. "Mommy die?" she asked. The big question. I turned around and faced her and then I looked at Don's profile as he drove, the tension in his jaw, his eyes staring straight ahead. I looked back at Rebecca and said, "No." I meant it. This disease was not going to take two lives.

Doctor Judi got clearance from Swedish Hospital to operate there. She also successfully argued my case before the ethics committee at her Catholic hospital, and was given permission to perform the therapeutic abortion to "save the life of the mother." I took this as another sign that the abortion was all right with God. I had already received the blessings of my pastors at Hope Lutheran Church and the members of my very fundamentally Christian family.

At noon the next day, Don and I returned to Swedish Hospital, to the very same waiting bay. Hours passed, waiting. Sometimes I softly cried; most of the time, Don and I sat in silence. He didn't dare leave for fear that I'd be gone when he got back. I wanted this ordeal to be over, but at the same time, I wanted every possible extra minute with the life inside me. We had named the baby David Eugene Sharp after our fathers. I talked to him silently, blessing him and loving him.

It was nearly seven o'clock when the attendant finally came with the gurney to take me to the operating room. I refused the ride. I wanted to walk. After all, I was going to an execution. Two things growing in me were going to die: a baby and a cancer.

It was the longest walk of my life. Silently, we rode down in the elevator, me in my hospital gown, Don on one side and the attendant on the other, surrounded by oblivious visitors and staff. We walked through one long corridor after another, deep into the bowels of the hospital.

We arrived at the operating room. Don disappeared behind swinging doors after I was put on a gurney and wheeled into another room. Intravenous needles were taped to my forearms. Anesthesia began to drip into one of the IV tubes; in moments, I would be unconscious. I looked up into the masked face of an anesthesiologist. "I've changed my mind," I tried to say. "I want my baby. I want my baby." I wasn't sure if the words I was speaking were being heard. Tears spilled from the anesthesiologist's eyes, leaving a wet trail down his mask. Then darkness fell.

Margaret Burrell had a dream that night. She dreamed that

AFTER THE LIGHT

I was bent over in a kneeling position in total darkness. I was crying so inconsolably that I did not notice one angel after another drifting down by my side, carrying illumination like soft, warm, night lights. One by one, they arrived to comfort me, completely enveloping me in their wings and their arms.

CHAPTER FOURTEEN

RE-MISSION

▼

D ARKNESS GAVE WAY to light, brilliant light. I opened
my eyes to the snow-covered face of Mount Rainier,
which seemed to float outside a wall of glass. Still groggy
from the anesthesia, I surveyed a huge, U-shaped room with enormous sprays of flowers covering every flat surface, a queen-size
sofa bed, a kitchen, a bar, and a private bathroom. What kind of
Caesar's Palace hospital was this?

Painfully, I shifted my body. A big thick bandage bulged beneath the hospital gown on my left side, and my left arm rested
on a pillow. "Well, if I'm going to suffer," I thought, "guess I'm
going to suffer in style."

A nurse entered the room. "Where am I?" I asked through a
dry, sticky mouth. "You're in the VIP suite," she answered. I
dozed off again.

I awakened to the grinning faces of Don, my mother, Rebecca, and Andy. "Not a bad place!" Don exclaimed.

"How did I get here?" I asked.

"I don't have a clue, hon. You might want to ask God."

Instead, I asked Dr. Brian Goodell, the medical director of
Swedish. Brian and I went way back to the days when he was a
young attending physician at Harborview. I used to see his cancer

patients on my own time because Brian's service did not have a social worker. He also founded the terminal illness seminar which I helped teach at the University of Washington School of Medicine. When we had talked on the phone prior to my surgery, I'd remarked that I hoped I would get a room with a view. Did I ever. It was a good illustration of my credo: Always be nice to everybody. You never know when that niceness is going to come back.

The first phase of my recovery went well. By the third day, I was out of bed with camera in hand, trying to take a picture of Mt. Rainier from my window. The mountain looked like a huge floating pink breast in the fading light of sunset. I had to have a photo because otherwise, no one would believe that I was being greeted each evening by a fourteen-thousand-foot breast in the sky. I waited until the light was perfect, then I began angling for my knockout shot.

The only way to take the picture I wanted was to rest the camera on an inside window ledge with the lens flush against the glass. But the sofa bed was in the way, so I couldn't get close enough to look through the view finder. I decided to squeeze between the couch and the window. Dragging my IV pole and assorted apparatus with me, I inched my way sideways into the narrow space. When I bent down to frame the shot, my hospital gown came undone in the back and slipped down on my arms and hands. I shrugged it off, letting it slide along the IV tubing while I took the picture. But when I tried to retrieve the gown, I couldn't reach it in that tight space. Then the IV tube snagged on something, and I was trapped.

There I was, bent over buck naked in front of a picture window for all to see. This was so ridiculous, I began to laugh. At that moment, two doors on opposite sides of my mammoth room opened. My mother entered one, bearing cans of soda from downstairs. A silver-haired stranger stood in the other. He turned out to be the head of the surgery department and was absolutely pop-eyed at the spectacle I presented.

My laughter was contagious. My mom began to laugh, too. She laughed so hard, she had to sit down. Tears of mirth ran down my face. I caught my breath and gasped, "Help me! I'm stuck!" That sent my mother and me into more gales of hysterical laughter. It was some time before I recovered my dignity and my gown and got back into bed.

The relentless pain I was feeling wasn't so funny. I couldn't seem to get away from it, even with medication. Don spent every night with me and heard me moaning in my sleep. Both he and my mother asked the doctors for higher and more frequent doses of medication, to no avail. The combination of pain, grief, and the hormonal aftereffects of pregnancy sent me into a deep depression on the day I was to be discharged from the hospital.

Almost as if I had paged her, my friend Teresa Carew—one of the Hens—came to see me. She sized up the situation immediately and told me that what I needed was a shower. I disagreed. I still had a tube in the side of my chest and I felt like I'd been pummeled. I was weak, tired, and listless. I hadn't had a shower since two days before surgery, and frankly, couldn't have cared less about getting clean.

Teresa ignored my protests and pushed me into the bathroom, IV pole and all. "Remove your gown," she instructed. I stood before her naked, with my bandages and tubes, thinking how I used to be a modest person. She turned on the water, got the temperature just right, and positioned me in the shower. She came at me with soap and washcloth and scrubbed every inch of my body, head to toe. I emerged dripping wet, shining clean, and smiling. Teresa was right; it did make me feel much better.

A few days after I got home, Henry Kaplan called with the

biopsy results. I was sitting in the kitchen talking with my mother and my friend Mary McKinney when the phone rang. "Kim," said Dr. Kaplan, not even bothering to identify himself, "it's zero nodes." Zero nodes. That meant the cancer hadn't spread to my lymph nodes after all.

In my shock, I could say nothing. My mother and Mary looked at my stricken face in alarm, assuming the worst. Finally, I repeated what he'd said. "It's no nodes." Then louder: "It's no nodes!" Then shouting: *"It's no nodes!"*

Mary and my mom embraced and danced around the room. I heard Dr. Kaplan say, "We have a medical term for this, Kim."

"What's that?" I asked.

There was a dramatic pause. "Miracle," he said.

I knew how the miracle had occurred. Prayers were being said for me twenty-four hours a day all around the world. Don and I had friends on almost every continent on earth. Many of them were part of prayer circles or participated in other forms of organized prayer and they made sure my name was said aloud as prayers were being offered from their church or group. At Nancy Evans Bush's church, I was on a list of people needing prayer which was read aloud every hour by prayer volunteers. My parents, my brother and his family, my sister and her family, and my Uncle Dean in Chicago all belonged to prayer circles. My own church in West Seattle, Hope Lutheran, as well as the parochial-school classrooms of Andy and Jennifer, prayed for me every morning.

I needed all the help I could get. On the last day of January, still bedridden and racked with pain, I noticed blood in the lymph fluid coming from my Jackson-Pratt drain. This was a temporary opening in my side to drain off excess lymphatic fluid, a task normally handled by the lymph glands, which of course were no longer there. Any interruption of this process could cause lymphedema, a painful and sometimes permanent swelling of the entire arm.

I called the doctor, but he was in surgery. Though I asked the receptionist to have him call me back, I didn't explain why. That was a mistake. Had I told her the nature of my call, I would have been instructed to see the next available surgeon immediately. Bleeding from the drain is a bad sign.

While I was waiting for the doctor to call, Joyce Hawkes dropped by for a visit. I knew Joyce from Seattle IANDS. She had been a research scientist in biophysics when a large leaded-glass window fell on her one day and crushed her skull. Joyce had a near-death experience which left her with the capacity to transmit energy. She ultimately left her academic job and became a fulltime healer.

Joyce sat cross-legged on the bed next to me as we watched bloody fluid pass through the drain tube. I complained about the pain, about the doctor not being available, about the bleeding. Joyce said, "You know I can help you, but my belief is that I need to be asked first."

Whoa, duh, Kim, I thought to myself. It was suddenly so obvious.

"Hey, Joyce, can you help with the pain and bleeding from my side?" I quickly asked.

"Yes," Joyce answered. She placed both hands above the site of the incision and the place where the tubes left my body. There was no mumbo jumbo, no strange ritual—in fact, we continued to chat. Deep penetrating heat came from her hands. I watched the color of the lymphatic fluid change from blood red to clear champagne, its normal hue. The pain, though not entirely gone, began to feel manageable. Joyce kept her hands in place.

Suddenly, my bedroom door was thrown open. There stood pint-size Rebecca, in a fury. Glaring at Joyce, she stomped across the room, struggled up on top of the bed, and marched across the mattress until her angry little face was just inches from Joyce's own. I was embarrassed. Rebecca was usually a pleasant, easy-going toddler. But Joyce understood completely. "Here is a very spiritual, very protective little being," she said admiringly. "I'm in her territory and she knows it."

Shortly after Joyce left, the surgeon returned my call and told me to come right in, even though the bleeding had already stopped. Gathering up to leave, I glanced at the lymph fluid collection bag and noticed a small dark object floating inside. It looked almost like a mouse. The doctor examined it and said it was an enormous blood clot, which had been the cause of the bleeding. How it had managed to squeeze through the small tubing into the bag, where it caused no further problems, the doctor didn't know. But I did.

Pain, pain, pain. I couldn't get rid of it. Begging for more pain medication made me feel like an addict or a hypochondriac. I knew the doctor didn't believe that I hurt as much as I said, but I was miserable. It showed, too. When I visited Dr. Kaplan for my first post-op oncology exam, he looked me over and said, "You look like dog meat."

That's what I loved about this guy—he told the truth. I told him about the pain that continued to plague me.

"You just have to get on top of the pain, Kim," he said matter-of-factly. "It shouldn't be hard and it shouldn't take long." He wrote out a prescription for Tylox, a potent pain reliever, and he wasn't stingy with the pills, either. He told me to take one or more, every four hours, whether I was in pain or not. The idea was to stay ahead of the pain, to stop the sensations before they got started. It worked. I weaned myself off the Tylox in fewer than twenty pills and got rid of the pain, too. Even more important than the relief was the fact that at last someone had heard me, had believed me, and treated me accordingly.

Dr. Kaplan had good news and bad news on the cancer front. The good news was that pathology reports showed that no cancer cells remained in my body—surgery had gotten it all. The bad news was that he wanted me to start chemotherapy.

We had gone round and round about this already. I did not want chemotherapy. I knew from my experience at the Hutch what the devastating effects of chemo were and I didn't feel I was the kind of person who could meet that kind of physical challenge. But there was another reason I was resisting Kaplan's advice. I knew chemotherapy was effective because it attacked every fast-growing cell in the body: not only tumor cells but hair cells, bone marrow cells, digestive tract cells, reproductive organ cells. At my age, chemo would render me sterile; I would probably go into premature menopause. This was the last thing I wanted. I had just lost a baby. Call me unrealistic, but I still hoped to have another one. I couldn't bear to give up that dream forever.

Dr. Kaplan kept arguing with me. "Look," he said. "You had an unusually deadly form of tumor material inside you. One tiny fraction of a cell can still be floating around in your body, and that would be enough to take your life. Chemotherapy would significantly improve your chances of not having a recurrence."

Finally, I gave in. I would do the chemo, but only the most conservative treatment available. And I wouldn't start until the day after Valentine's Day. Dr. Kaplan's eyebrows shot up quizzically. I explained that every year on Valentine's Day, Don and I returned to the elegant restaurant where we'd gotten engaged. I didn't want to miss that dinner or throw it up. This also gave me another eleven days to psych myself up for six months of being poisoned. Kaplan agreed to those conditions and we shook on it.

It gave me a heady sense of power, being in control of what happened to my body—especially since my body had so recently been out of my control. Until this conversation with Dr. Kaplan, I had been acting like a passive recipient to whatever a doctor said in regard to my health care. I had even been reticent to insist on medication to ease the pain that was driving me crazy. To heck with that attitude. I was stepping up to the plate as an active player in the game.

The experience of the next day reinforced that determination. I went with Don to a surgeon's office for removal of the Jackson-Pratt drain. Because the nurse who made the appointment for me mentioned the nasty word—*procedure*—I made a mental note to pop a Tylox before I went in.

At the doctor's office, I soon found myself wishing I'd taken a whole handful of Tylox. The only prepping the surgeon gave me was telling me to look at Don. When I turned my head, he gave a mighty pull on the tube. It hurt so badly I almost passed out. Dizzy with pain, I saw the surgeon holding a device about the size of a lawn sprinkler.

"Shouldn't I have had anesthesia for this or some kind of warning?" I asked.

"Nah," he said. "You'll have forgotten the pain by the time you get to your car."

I wanted to shove the lawn sprinkler down his throat. Let him try to get it out without pain medication. I marched out of the office. The site of the drain removal felt like a small dog was biting me until the next morning.

I started chemotherapy with my hair freshly frosted a glorious ice-blond shade. You could view that as either a sign of extreme optimism—or foolishness. The fact was I had always been vain about my thick mane, my pride and joy. If it was going to fall out, I at least wanted it looking its best.

My chemo treatments began with an intravenous infusion of Methotrexate and Fluorouracil, commonly known as 5-FU. The chemicals went in cold but comfortably. Within moments, my mouth was filled with their metallic taste. When I got home, I made a big black X over the date on the countdown calendar that I had hung in the bathroom. Only twenty-five more weeks to go.

The next morning was harder. I was starting oral Cytoxan, one of the most nauseating chemical compounds used in chemotherapy. The little gray pill lay on the bathroom counter next to the sink while I tried to gather the courage to take it. Minutes passed. I got down on my knees so that it was at eye-level, and I began talking to it as if it could hear me. "I love you," I said, not meaning a word of it. "You're going to save my life. I'm going to really enjoy taking you every morning for the next six months." What a crock this was, I thought. On the other hand, I couldn't deny how lucky I was to have a pill at all. I knew AIDS patients who would happily swallow ground glass if it would help. Feeling grateful, I put the little gray pill in my mouth and swallowed.

That night, my bed became a rocking ship tossed from one wave of fire to another. Below deck, I was unable to get a breath of fresh air. The ship got caught in a whirlpool, around and around, faster and faster, until it went down. I woke up, stumbled into the bathroom, leaned over the toilet, and barfed my brains out. I was sick over and over again; then I gagged with the dry heaves. The room kept spinning and the fire kept burning and the retching wouldn't stop. The only relief I could get was by lying down on the cold marble floor of the entryway downstairs, where I stayed until morning.

By the third week of chemo, I had "lost" my blood veins in

the crook of my arm where I received the chemicals intravenously each Friday. What next? Plan A was to get a central line, a small catheter that fits under the skin near the collar bone and allows direct access into a vein. I flat out refused—not only because it required more surgery but because it would be permanent. I wanted no lasting memory, other than the hook-shaped scar on the side of my left breast, that any of this had ever happened to me. Instead, I went with Plan B, which was to receive chemotherapy through a needle into a vein on the back of my hand. Dr. Kaplan said if that failed, they would put a needle between my fingers, then they would try between my toes, then directly into my neck, and then into my scalp. "Enough!" I cried. "Let's start with the hand."

My first meeting with my breast cancer support group was totally depressing. There were about fourteen of us, and we introduced ourselves to one another by briefly describing our diagnosis and treatment. The stories got worse and worse as we went around the table. I was the next-to-last to talk, and everyone was aghast when I told about losing the baby. Then the last woman told us that not only did she have cancer, but so did her nine-year-old son. We were all in tears, and left feeling miserable.

I couldn't stand the thought of returning. I didn't want to know these women. I didn't want their problems to become part of my life. But I was also committed to the group and truly believed we were there to help one another. I started thinking about what I could do to contribute, and I seized upon the idea of wacky hats. At a costume shop, I bought a different silly hat for each of the six weeks of group therapy. At our next meeting—a serious occasion because we got a lecture on radiation—I wore a beret with two antennalike coiled springs that burst from a headband. At the end of the coils were large, glitter-covered styrofoam balls which sent sparkles flying in all directions with every move of my head. It brought just the right touch of humor and lunacy into the group.

Each weekend after a Friday chemo infusion, I felt like I had a terrible case of the flu. By Monday, I would be OK, but the anticipation of being violently ill every weekend was conditioning me to want to avoid chemo. I called Joyce Hawkes and asked if she could help. She came over to my house one day after the weekly infusion. I lay on the couch and closed my eyes as her hands passed over my body, emanating heat. I could actually feel something being suctioned from my chest and belly. Then I heard a choir, a chorus of angel voices singing a song of praise and thanks, a song of creation. I had never heard the likes of it, not even in my near-death experience. I felt that I was somehow hearing a song that surrounded me always—and not just me, but all of us, the entire planet, the universe and beyond. It was beautiful beyond description.

My eyes flew open in wondrous surprise, and I saw that the look on Joyce's face mirrored my own. The choir faded into silence as we looked at each other in awe. Finally, almost tentatively, Joyce asked, "Did you hear that?" "Yes," I replied. Even though the chorus lasted only a few moments, we knew the memory of this unearthly harmony would last a lifetime. And I spent the entire weekend without a trace of nausea.

In mid-March, my doctors decided to begin radiation treatments as well. The standard protocol for women with breast cancer who had not had a full mastectomy was chemotherapy followed by radiation. Now there was new evidence that women who received radiation within twelve weeks of their cancer diagnosis had a reduced risk of recurrence. That meant starting radiation while chemo was still underway—a tremendous assault on the body. Because the combined treatment was still a relatively new technique, the doctors weren't sure what the effects would be, except that my skin would be more susceptible to burns, and I would become very tired.

In preparation, my chest was intricately marked with little dots of silver nitrate to show exactly where the radiation should be aimed. I then learned that the little dots would become permanent tattoos. "What!" I said, which was becoming my standard reaction each time I was told of the next unpleasant "procedure" that awaited me in my cancer treatment. "It's no big deal," assured the technician. "The tattoos will be in the same place as your dots. They'll be itty-bitty, but they have to be permanent in case there's another time in your life when someone considers giving you radiation in the same area."

My tattoo session was scheduled for the next day, April 1, one of my high holidays. I had to do something. On my left breast, with a red magic marker, I wrote WRONG BOOB in enormous letters. Underneath, in smaller black letters I wrote, APRIL FOOLS.

At the Tumor Institute, I waited in a treatment room wearing a poker face and the usual hospital gown. A male technician— why are they always men?—came in with the tatooing instruments. He was a serious, sober man who greeted me with professional briskness before getting down to work. He untied my gown to expose my chest and stared, wordlessly, at my handiwork. His expression never changed. He closed the gown, excused himself, and stepped outside the room. I heard hysterical laughter coming from the other side of the door. Then he composed himself, returned, and with the same sober expression asked if he could bring others in to see me. "Sure, why not?" I said, wondering if I should solicit tips. A parade of radiation technicians filed merrily by, laughing their heads off. Someone took a few headless photos with a Polaroid. Snapshots of my naked April Fools' chest are probably still decorating bulletin boards somewhere in the Tumor Institute.

*   *   *

Humor, prayer, healing touch—you name it, I used it. Some-times, I received the laying on of hands by Christian friends or family members, and sometimes, healers visited me at home to give me their own particular brand of healing energy. On other occasions, I received Therapeutic Touch, a nonreligious form of laying on of hands, from Doris Kunz, one of the developers of this form of therapy.

I consumed gallons of miso soup—it was the only hot food that tasted good to me. My sister-in-law, Julie Sharp, and her Japanese mother introduced me to homemade miso soup, made from scratch. Julie told me how the soup helped offset the dam-aging effects of radiation on the atom-bomb survivors of Hiro-shima and Nagasaki. Almost everything else I ingested during chemotherapy had to be ice cold. Unfortunately, most of those ice-cold foods were high in calories. I had anticipated that the one good side effect of chemotherapy and radiation would be weight loss. Instead, I packed on the ice-cream pounds.

I didn't lose all my blond hair, either—just enough fell out in big patches to look horrible. I tried to console myself with little indulgences, such as wearing beautiful silky pajamas and robes. This soon exploded into an expensive habit. I rationalized that I was more attractive to Don wearing a silk teddy as I threw up than wearing my usual flannel nighties.

The bulk of my radiation treatment ended in mid-May. I girded myself for the grand finale—a ten-day burst of intense radiation that was supposed to finish off any remnants of the tumor for good. My left breast already looked like raw meat and the radiation burns took on a deep-purple hue. Wearing a bra was intolerable. Out of mercy, my doctors pulled me completely off Methotrexate, the ingredient in my chemo that was primarily responsible for the breaking down of my skin tissue.

By the end of May, I was at my nadir, feeling the cumulative effects of combined chemo and radiation. Nausea and fatigue clung to me like a choking cloud. I was bleeding from the radiation site and still losing hair in clumps. Then I saw a TV special about breast cancer and I was reminded that I wasn't alone. In my pity party I had forgotten that so many of us around the world dealing with cancer struggle over the same issues of fear, despair, hope, appreciation of life—all the things one feels when confronted with a life-threatening illness or any seemingly overwhelming challenge.

How blessed I felt to have had a near-death experience so I didn't have to deal with the existential fear of death, on top of my other fears and concerns. For many people a diagnosis of a potentially terminal illness results in a paralyzing fear of death. It interferes with their recovery. In some cases it may actually impede it. I decided right then and there to stop complaining. I was going to take all the energy left over from not being afraid of death, and apply it to getting well.

I focused on plans that had been interrupted by my cancer diagnosis and treatment. With renewed vigor, I threw myself into my responsibilities as chairperson of the Pacific Northwest conference on near-death studies. I helped my sister plan a large family reunion in Kansas City at the end of the summer. I decided to attend the twenty-fifth reunion of my high school graduating class—and I toilet trained Rebecca.

In July, as the radiation burns began to fade, my surgeon examined me and proclaimed, "Breast cancer surgery doesn't get any better than this." He later took many pictures of my chest to prove it. On our wedding night at the Inn at the Market in Seattle, Don and I had clinked our champagne glasses and vowed to return to this same room five years later. With the long ordeal of cancer treatment just ending by the time of our fifth wedding anniversary, we settled for driving by and waving at the hotel room from our car. Such is the unpredictable journey of life.

During the first week of August, Don and I and the children went to Kansas for the twenty-fifth reunion of the Shawnee Mission East High School Class of 1966. It was my first high school reunion. Of course, I wanted to look gorgeous, successful, well-rested, youthful, fit, etc., and generally make a fabulous impression. Instead, I was nauseated, exhausted, ugly, gray, weak, flabby, and wormy-feeling. That's what I saw in the mirror of my childhood bedroom as I prepared to join my exclassmates for an evening of rollicking fun.

As I spread body makeup all over to give an artificially healthy tone to my pallid skin, my thoughts drifted to my favorite saying: "Before enlightenment, chop wood, carry water. After enlightenment, chop wood, carry water." In other words, spiritually enlightened though we all may become, our earthly responsibilities will always await us. But we can infuse that work with spirituality and gratitude and praise for the Creator that made it all possible.

Ever so carefully, so as to lose as few strands as possible, I unwound the curlers from my still-frosted blond hair. My thoughts drifted. What had I learned in all these years since I drove out of Kansas? I had learned to walk in faith. I learned that faith is the greatest gift God has given us. It's not an act of faith to see angels or have communication with deceased loved ones. It's faith when we believe in these things with absolutely no evidence of their existence. That is one of the great gifts of life—to sustain that faith against all odds, against critics and skeptics, against our own self-doubt.

I smoothed foundation over my face. I spread aquamarine eye shadow across my lids, and mascara upon the eyelashes that remained from chemotherapy. A cloud of powdered blush put pink in my cheeks. Faith, that's what this was all about. Faith that there is a purpose for our lives no matter who we are or what our circumstances. Faith that there is an invisibility full of characters, some who trip us up, some who keep us from falling down, some who guide us. Faith that our souls are eternal and will endure beyond our earthly existence.

I applied bright-red lipstick and clipped on sparkling earrings. I took my party dress off the hanger behind me, stepped into it, and pulled it on. It was a dress carefully chosen to accentuate the shapeliness of my legs and my cleavage. For me, cleavage was symbolic. I was proud of it. I wanted my old friends to see that I still had it. This was vanity, but it was also pluck. It was fed by my fire, the fire of my faith. Faith that there is meaning to our existence and that our day-to-day struggles count.

Slipping on my white high heels, I twirled in front of the mirror. Like a matador, I had been transformed by gilt and fabric. I went outside where Don was waiting for me by the car. I relished his long, low wolf whistle, his approval. His love had never left even when I had been at my sickest and sickest-looking. He knew the real me. He knew what was under the makeup and party dress and hair coloring and he still loved me. Entering a marriage, you never know for sure what will happen when the rubber hits the road, when trials and tribulations cloud the future. How blessed I felt, looking at Don and seeing his love for me reflected back.

As we drove to the first reunion gathering that Friday night, anxiety caught up with me. What if no one remembered me? What if everyone remembered me and wished I hadn't come? Typical fear-of-reunion stuff. I turned to thoughts of love. I thought of the Light which twice in my life had lifted me up, held me high, and carried me safely to the shore. The Light had taught me the meaning of love, which is that we are here to help each other, and that I wasn't finished loving or helping yet. I knew that. Although I did not fear death, I did not want to die, and was not ready to die. I had too much left to learn and too much left to teach. I had been returned to life for some purpose, and it wasn't to die of cancer. My purpose was to try and create the Light here. To be the Light as I saw and felt it—warm, loving, accepting—and to help light the way for others who have not been as lucky as I.

We pulled into the parking lot, got out of the car, and walked toward a knot of people gathered in front of the clubhouse where the party was being held. The very first person I saw was Bob Clark, whom I had once planned to marry a lifetime ago. He hadn't changed in all this time. Other friends came into view: Merrily and Lewie, Priscilla, Mark, Barbara, Lynne. I laughed. We were beginning to look like our parents.

Heads turned and there was joyful recognition on every face I saw. We squealed and screamed and hugged; kissed, laughed, cried. When at last we settled down, someone said to me, "Well, Kim, so what have you been up to?"

I took a deep breath. "You're not going to believe this," I said, "but in 1970, my dad and I were at the Department of Motor Vehicles in Shawnee Mission, and I started to feel really strange. . . ."

EPILOGUE

Spring 1995

▼

T HE INFORMATION compiled for *After the Light* was drawn
from my diaries, journals, calendars, appointment books,
patient charts, and interviews with old friends, many of
whom I had not communicated with in years. It was reconnecting
with these friends that was the most satisfying part of the preparation to write the book. Everyone I contacted validated my
memories of even the weirdest of events. All were doing superbly
well in interesting lives, so much so that I thought I would share
their progress—and mine—with you.

My happiest news is that I am in remission from cancer and
am four years into a ten-year span before Dr. Kaplan will use the
other "C" word, *cured.* Dr. Kaplan and Dr. Judi fact-checked the
cancer section of the book. I learned for the first time that several
of those attending me in surgery when I ended my pregnancy
wept—behavior almost unheard of in operating rooms. Dr. Judi
was struck by the incredible metaphor for threatened womanhood
that the simultaneous theurapeutic abortion and partial mastectomy represented. She's never forgotten that night.

After almost nine years of marriage, Don and I are continu-
ally grateful that we found each other. We're like many American
couples—we don't see each other nearly enough and we live pay-

check to paycheck. In 1984 Don was promoted to Lieutenant in the Seattle Fire Department and is one of the supervisors of Medic One. He has been our exclusive breadwinner since Rebecca's birth. We agree that right now my most important job in life is raising our children, who remain our greatest teachers.

My parents reconciled a few months after I moved to Seattle and are happily planning their fiftieth wedding anniversary. Dad retired as the senior partner in his law firm and Mom continues her interior decorating passion, usually on her own home—the same home I left in 1970. During the seventies, under different circumstances, they became born-again Christians.

Brother Paul is producing his fifteenth contemporary Christian record album. He married a neighbor girl he had known since the second grade and has four children. Besides touring, he is a songwriter and producer and is Worship Leader in his church.

Sister Kristy is still married to her childhood sweetheart and they live in the St. Louis area with their four children. We call them "the little people"; when they married they joked that they were so short that they earned their honeymoon money by hiring themselves out as the bride and groom on other people's wedding cakes. Kristy is Director of Bible Studies at a large nondenominational church.

Mary Sue Bollig dropped the "Mary" and most of her addresses since I last saw her. She has lived or traveled extensively in forty-nine states and twenty countries. She currently lives in Hawaii and is pursuing a master's degree in art therapy with children.

My "haunted house"-mates are in various stages of domestication. Laurie Gates focused her social work practice in the field of community mental health until her second child was born. She is a full-time wife and mom in suburban Portland, Oregon. Christy Horton lives in the countryside north of Seattle with her horses and dogs. She is a physician in emergency medicine and is avidly pursuing spiritual interests. Marsha Miller lives in Maryland with her husband and two children and works as an administrative assistant in cardiology at a world famous Baltimore medical center.

Kenny Brown more than fulfilled the promise of God's blessing that afternoon when we watched the ferry. Despite increasing health problems, he, with his guide dog at his side, devoted his life to the Boy Scouts of America organization. His brother Ron, who has a successful psychiatric practice in Seattle, reported that Kenny died three years ago and is buried in a Boy Scout wilderness reserve next to a memorial built in his honor.

In May of 1994 I returned to Columbus, Ohio, for the first time since George Koestner's death. He is buried with his grandfather, who died not too long after George. Given the fact that George visited me after his death, I was amused at the irony that his cemetery is outside of Shadeville, down the road from Lazurus.

Margaret Kapualani Burrell has integrated her near-death experience and other spiritual influences into her extensive Pacific Rim infant massage and Lomi Lomi courses. She has not had a dream vision about me since the night the angels comforted me.

Joyce Hawkes has developed a full-time healing/teaching practice in Bellevue, Washington. Her God-given gift of healing continues to increase.

My three fellow NDErs and co-founders of Seattle IANDS have gone through major transitions. Joan Berryman, the quintessential scientist, is director of religious education at her church and has completed a chaplaincy program specializing in children and cancer. Betty Preston has survived two cherished husbands and lives in a senior care facility. Her memory has failed alarmingly but she easily remembers every detail of her near-death experience. I last saw Caroline Graves in poor health at a local nursing home. Because she is no longer listed there as a resident, I assume that at last she crossed the chasm and reunited with her beloved relatives.

There are many people mentioned in the book with whom I have utterly lost contact, most notably Maria. She moved to Seattle after her hospitalization, where for years I regularly saw her at Harborview's cardiology clinic. When I returned from Europe in 1980 she was nowhere to be found. I don't even remember her last name. Who knew it would one day be so important to have her validate her out-of-body experience? And that tennis shoe is probably somewhere in our garage, which is like saying it's as accessible as the Ark of the Covenant in the warehouse scene at the end of *Raiders of the Lost Ark*.

Fortunately, I have kept much better track of Vicki Umipeg, the only blind-since-birth NDE'r I have ever met. She was born prematurely in 1950 and was immediately placed in one of the newly developed air-lock incubators. This device provided extra oxygen, but also destroyed Vicki's optic nerves. Since then she has seen nothing. Even her dreams contain no visual data, just other sensations such as touch and sound. Here is her story:

> Though blind, I worked as a singer and pianist at a restaurant in Seattle. On February 2, 1973, I reluctantly accepted a ride home from a drunk couple, and near the base of Queen Anne hill our van crashed. My first awareness after that was of being near the ceiling at Harborview Hospital. I could see! In this abbreviated account of that evening, it may sound as though I had my act together. But it was so amazing to *see* that it was a complication in my efforts to cope.
>
> Below me hospital personnel were discussing how I might be in a vegetative state. I was frustrated and angry

because to them it was like I didn't even exist! I just wanted to get out of there. Almost immediately, as if in response to my thought, I was drawn up through the hospital, and was rising through space. I felt so free! In the distance I heard the most beautiful sound, like wind chimes. As a musician I was awed. There were so many different tones that I didn't know were possible!

Then I was sucked head first into a dark tunnel, drawn by a wind toward a far-off light. I felt a whooshing feeling as though giant fans drew me. Near the end of the tunnel the light became brilliant and I ended up rolling onto the grass of a bright land of trees and flowers, where there were thousands of people singing, talking and laughing. I can't describe the colors there, because I still have no sense of what color is, but everywhere there were dazzling shades of light. The flowers, which I recognized from their scent, and the birds, from their sound, also seemed to have light around them. Towards me came Debby and Diane, two friends I had known at the Oregon State School for the Blind who had died while I was attending there.

Then, for an instant, it seemed as if I knew everything, that everything made sense. Suddenly I intuitively understood math and science, and I don't know beans about math and science. I *hadn't asked* about calculus. Now I understood it. As Debby and Diane approached, I sensed a boundary across which I could not go. Then Christ appeared, and I was enveloped in His Love. His light filled my vision. Holding out a raised right hand toward me, He said very definitely, "No!," preventing us from touching each other. His face was strong and kind. He could see everything about me, more than I could see

239

0-595-28028-5

Lightning Source UK Ltd.
Milton Keynes UK
13 January 2010

148568UK00001B/24/A